# Love's Playbook V

## The Advantage of Weakness

### Exodus 1-24

Arla Caraboolad

Copyright: February 2017

ISBN: 13: 978-1544106236

ISBN-10: 1544106238

By Arla Caraboolad

Wind Words Publishing

To Abba, Adonai and Ruach for believing in me.

And to Oprah who challenged me to study "…a jealous God visiting the iniquities of the fathers upon the children…"

# Contents

Introduction ..........................................................................13

**Chapter 1** .........................................................................17

*It's Time!*...........................................................................17
    Exodus 1 ......................................................................17

**Chapter 2** .........................................................................24

*The Deliverer*......................................................................24
    Exodus 2:1-9 ...............................................................24

**Chapter 3** .........................................................................32

*Moses Gets Ready*................................................................32
    Exodus 2:10-15.............................................................32

**Chapter 4** .........................................................................46

*"Now What?"*.......................................................................46
    Exodus 2:15-20.............................................................46

**Chapter 5** .........................................................................55

*God Provides* ......................................................................55
    Exodus 2:21 ...............................................................55

**Chapter 6** .........................................................................67

*Wasted Time?*......................................................................67
    Exodus 2:21-3:1............................................................67

**Chapter 7** .........................................................................77

*God Makes an Appearance*....................................................77
    Exodus 3:1-4:19............................................................77

**Chapter 8** .........................................................................87

*Surprises along the Way* ......................................................87

Exodus 4:20-28 ........................................................ 87

**Chapter 9** .......................................................... **103**

*Going Home* ............................................................ *103*
Exodus 4:29-6:30 .................................................. 103

**Chapter 10** ........................................................ **115**

*The Spiritual Battle Intensifies* ................................. *115*
Exodus 7:1-8:19 ................................................... 115

**Chapter 11** ........................................................ **125**

*Lord of the Flies* ...................................................... *125*
Exodus 8:20-24 .................................................... 125

**Chapter 12** ........................................................ **135**

*Would God Do That?* .............................................. *135*
Exodus 8:21-9:35 .................................................. 135

**Chapter 13** ........................................................ **145**

*The Power Struggle Ends* .......................................... *145*
Exodus 10:1-12:29 ................................................ 145

**Chapter 14** ........................................................ **155**

*"Get Out!"* .............................................................. *155*
Exodus 12:30-14:4 ................................................ 155

**Chapter 15** ........................................................ **167**

*"Stand Still and See!"* ................................................ *167*
Exodus 14:5-15:21 ................................................ 167

**Chapter 16** ........................................................ **181**

*Already?* .................................................................. *181*
Exodus 15:22—16:31 ............................................. 181

**Chapter 17** ..................................................................**193**

*Not Again!* ..................................................................*193*

Exodus 17 ..................................................................193

**Chapter 18** ..................................................................**201**

*Reunited* ..................................................................*201*

Exodus 18:1-19:16 ..................................................................201

**Chapter 19** ..................................................................**211**

*The Awesome Covenant* ..................................................................*211*

Exodus 19:16--Exodus 20:22 ..................................................................211

**Chapter 20** ..................................................................**223**

*Blessed Beyond Belief* ..................................................................*223*

Exodus 20:22-24:18 ..................................................................223

# Acknowledgments

Greatest thanks goes to God for trusting me with telling Their story in truth and making them look good "with no darkness at all" (1 John 1:5, and all through the Psalms They are declared all good).

Every time I start a new episode I wonder if I can do it. But Ruach always whispers courage and every one I write becomes my new favorite.

Also thanks to my husband who listens and listens, and honestly tells me when they need to be redone. Your input is so valuable. Your patience so appreciated.

My friend Barb has been such an encouragement. I think she is more excited about this series than I am! Her enthusiasm has been a reviving cooling breeze in what at times feels like a desert of obscurity and discouragement.

And finally thanks to Oprah who voiced her feelings about a "jealous" God that was the catalyst to begin studying it.

# Introduction

In this fourth episode God raises up a man to take Jacob's family, now a large nation, out of Egypt to the land He promised Abraham.

Archaeology hasn't caught up with this yet. They haven't been able to find any record that looks anything like two million or more people leaving Egypt. But according to Timothy Mahoney, whose excellent film I saw on Netflix shortly before publishing this episode, they are hung up on the word Ramses in Exodus 1:11 as establishing the date of the exodus in Ramses reign. Mahoney went with searching out patterns and the biblical date in 1Kings 6:1, and found a wealth of evidence 200 years earlier. His film is "Patterns of Evidence Exodus," and is amazing. Ramses II renamed Tanis after him (formerly it was called Avaris by the Hyksos). A later copyist updated the name of the city in scripture. It's that simple.

Archaeology didn't find a record of King David until 1993, so we shouldn't be surprised if some of these things stay hidden for the time being.

What is getting clearer, with every passing episode, is when God wants to lead a man to something big; They[1] first call him away from family and culture to a time alone with Them. Sometimes it is many years until the fulfilment of Their plan. It takes time to unlearn the programming we have. And usually what makes sense to us is our power. We value strength.

God, however, has shown again and again that They are looking for a trust relationship. If you have read episode three, you saw what value God places on relationship with us. And if this is your first episode, in these stories God is a position—one God, to be sure—made up of three beings: Eloah Elohim usually referred to as Abba, Adonai Elohim sometimes appearing as the Angel of the Lord (Michael), and Ruach Elohim, aka the Holy Spirit. Because if God values anything, it is relationship.

These are the Bible stories written with Biblical research and imagination from a cosmic perspective. You will read about conversations God has amongst Themselves (some of them in scripture), and conversations They have with

---

[1] See the next paragraph for thinking of God as plural: "Elohim" (Gen. 1:1) is plural.

people—there in scripture, but I just read over them without realizing their importance, or how involved God is and how much They want to be with humans. Also, just by implication, we have a huge audience watching the unfolding of the drama here on earth.

I always ask for Ruach's wisdom and help to stay true to the ideas and stories of scripture. After writing five of these, it strikes me that God has to educate the people They use, because typically we have our own ideas of how it should be done. We have a terrible time waiting on God to do it Their way, and we often make things worse by "helping" God. So I am very aware of my dependence on Them. But this will be a different perspective—I am a female and a mental health (family systems) therapist.

Also, if you are new to this view, you will notice there is definitely a dark side headed by God's arch enemy Satan (meaning "the accuser" or "the adversary") who is very busy trying to prove to the on-looking universe that God is not good and not fit to be their ruler. He also claims that humans are irredeemable. The dark side consists of the angels he deceived and took with him when God set a boundary on their lie-spreading. They blame God for all the suffering and pain here. It is a little like Chess with many moves and counter moves between powers of good and powers of evil. And we can see them continuing today. God allows this demonstration of truth because They want evidence to base the security of the universe on— more than Their word against the dark side's word.

Enjoy! And if you haven't read the others, and want the full story, read episodes 1-4. May Ruach be with you and give you an experience of God's goodness and majesty.

Chapter 1

# It's Time!

## Exodus 1

*God is never in a hurry,*

*but They are always on time.*

Back at the sheep ranch in Goshen, Egypt with the other side of Job's family, you will remember Jacob's kids moved to Egypt and were thriving when we left them. Because of Joseph, they have been supported by Pharaoh, and never suffered throughout the five remaining years of famine. In fact, they are proliferating. Life is good.

Everyone else in Egypt belonged to the king when the famine was over. The Egyptians had sold everything they had for food, and finally themselves, so they wouldn't die. Many of them came close to death, and they certainly weren't reproducing by the end. But Joseph had been wise in allowing the Egyptians to buy back their freedom in exchange for 1/5 of their produce each year after the famine. So while they are still paying 20% in taxes to the king, they are, at least, not Pharaoh's slaves.

The Israelites, on the other hand, being honored for Joseph's sake have flourished, having every want supplied. They have no taxes, as do the Egyptians, and they are free. They had nothing in common with the Egyptians in culture, religion or lifestyle, and have maintained the separateness between them. The clean-shaven Egyptians are afraid of getting lice, and think shepherds are dirty, second-class people. They have beards!

One hundred years pass, Joseph has been dead for almost 30 years. His brothers are all dead too. But their descendants are alive and well in Egypt, having a population explosion!

Then comes into power a Pharaoh who has no personal knowledge of Joseph. In fact, he doesn't want to hear any more about Joseph and how wonderful he was, and what great things he and his God did for Egypt. He had heard it all his life, and he doesn't care to hear more. Egyptians have taken back the throne, and Thutmose I, son of Amenhotep I, has come into power. He is a proud

Egyptian, forward thinking, and wants to make a name for himself. He notices how rapidly the Israelite race is growing, and he decides something must be done. He can't banish them by law. *And besides*, he thinks, *that would be foolish; they will make a wonderful workforce for my projects*. And Thutmose I begins scheming.

He will have to carry his counselors with him, and so calls his cabinet and addresses them, "Have you noticed how rapidly the Israelites are increasing and how capable they are? We need to make a plan to deal wisely with them or they will soon outnumber us. And in case of war, they may join our enemies, or leave with them."

He proposes his plan to build cities and use their talent and expertise. His counselors approve his work projects; Pharaoh has two cities he wants to build, Pithom and Tanis (later named Rameses).

## Cosmic Influence

Satan was the mastermind behind this and I'm sure Pharaoh was flattering to the Israelites in the beginning—saying how they needed their talent and expertise—even paying them. But it isn't long before more and more are hired, until all the Hebrew males are conscripted. They all have masters over them and work becomes more menial and less pleasant. The constant tending of the Nile was required all year and was grueling work.

It is the king's plan to make them less prolific by their hard labor, whether in the field or building, but it seems to make them even more productive. He tells his taskmasters to be hard on them, but the worse they are treated, the more babies they have.

Finally Pharaoh becomes desperate and has the Hebrew midwives, Puah (splendor) and Shiphrah (beauty), called to him. "The Hebrews are having a population explosion," he tells them, and we can't allow your people to outnumber the Egyptians. When you go to the delivery of Hebrew women, as soon as you can see it's a boy, I want you to kill it. You can let the girls live."

Even though they have no children of their own, they are shocked and scandalized. They can no more agree to this than fly! But you don't say "no" to the king and live. So they bow, say, "Yes, your majesty," and leave.

"What is he thinking?" cries Puah when they are alone and off of palace grounds. "We can't do that!" She was young and horrified that the king could order such a thing.

20

"You are absolutely right!" said Shiphrah, "We are in the business of saving lives, not taking them. And we aren't going to! What would God think of us?"

"But what will we do?" wailed Puah. "Pharaoh will certainly find out and have us killed!"

"We'll just trust God, and keep doing what we are doing. Only we will go a little later when they call. And then we can tell him we didn't get there in time because they deliver so fast. That isn't a lie; they do deliver faster than Egyptian women. It will take him years to figure it out anyway."

Adonai and Ruach are pleased that the midwives hear Ruach's whispers, and choose to stand for right against the king.

"It's not easy to defy the most powerful one in the country," says Adonai to Ruach, love shining in His eyes.

"Yes," replies Ruach, "We don't have many who listen for Our words anymore since Jacob and Joseph are dead."

"Let's do something special for the two midwives who trusted Us and did the right thing without fear. Let's give them children of their own."

"Great idea!" responds Adonai smiling, a twinkle in his eye. "But first let's find a husband for Puah."

"Got it!" laughed Ruach, as he left on a mission.

### A New Plan

Quite frankly, the king, who is used to being obeyed, forgets about it. *That's handled*, he thinks. *I gave the orders myself.* And it is four years before he thinks of it again. (Aaron is three years older than Moses.)

Then one day, Satan plants an idea in Thutmose to ride out in his chariot to see how his new city (the one the Hebrews are building) is coming along. He notices an awfully lot of children running around. *How can this be?* He asks himself. *There should only be little girls, but I see many boys!*

He doesn't waste any time calling for the midwives again, who are scared out of their minds. But they agree that they will say just what they had planned, and trust God to keep them safe.

"Why did you not obey my orders?" asks Pharaoh a little louder than necessary, when they are brought in before him.

Shiphrah and Puah are shaking, but the older one replies sounding quite calm and convincing. "Your majesty, the Hebrew women aren't like the

Egyptian women. They are more vigorous and quicker to give birth. By the time we get there, the baby is born, and we cannot kill them then!"

"I should never have trusted women with such an assignment! roars the king," the veins on his forehead bulging in anger. "I'll have my people throw all your baby boys in the Nile!" and he has them thrown out of his chambers. (And if there wasn't hatred between those races before, you can be sure it starts then. But at least he doesn't order the midwives to be killed.) Satan is scheming because he knows a deliverer is coming.

Badly shaken, the two women go home to hide their own boys and tell all their friends and neighbors to hide theirs.

You might imagine how the Israelites cry to God then. And Abba, Adonai and Ruach look at each other and say, "It's time!"

"Abraham's children have begun to suffer in Egypt," says Abba. "By the time We get them out, it will be intense. The Amorites have had almost four generations to decide for Us, and they haven't. It's time for a deliverer."

Chapter 2

# The Deliverer

## Exodus 2:1-9

*Again God spoils Satan's plan.*

If you are reading scripture along with this, you may wonder why Moses fails to mention his sister and brother in the first three verses of chapter 2, saying his father Amram married his mother Jochebed and they had Moses. The significant thing in his mind was that both parents were Levites, and he was born after the king's edict that all Hebrew baby boys were to be thrown into the Nile River.

Enter Moses. He is three years younger than his brother Aaron, so it is highly unlikely that his mother had been married before and had just then married his father. And an interesting side note: if the midwives had been afraid and had done as the Pharaoh ordered them to, Aaron wouldn't have survived. But he did.

And then along comes Moses. He is a beautiful baby with bright eyes, communicating with sounds and a smile before two months, and it is clear that he is highly intelligent.

His mother and father believe that God's promise of deliverance given to Abraham is about to be fulfilled. They have been prompted by Ruach as they look at the terrible state of affairs, and the pain of their people, and they wonder if this child might be Israel's chosen deliverer. He is the fourth generation from Abraham.

(Josephus says that God had revealed to Amram that Moses would lead Israel out of Egypt; although his source is not known.)[i]

Fortunately, Moses is good natured and rarely cries, making it easier to hide him as long as mama keeps his needs met. But after three months it is getting harder. Jochebed is not about to throw her baby in the river, nor let anyone else, but what will she do? She prays for wisdom, and in her imagination sees a baby floating in a basket.

That is all she needs. And she begins work on a basket that very afternoon. She makes it waterproof with tar and then clay, and when it is dry, she lines it with Moses' favorite blanket and lays him in it. It has a cover to keep the sun off of him, yet allowing him to breathe. She and Miriam take him down to the river and put the basket in the water, but she doesn't stay, afraid of endangering him or herself.

Miriam has been instructed exactly where to stay and not to get him if he cries, but to amuse herself playing by the river's edge where she can watch to see what happens. Jochebed knows that it is the princess' custom to bathe in that spot—possibly steps to a bathing pool had been built there for the royals. It was believed the Nile god gave fertility and life.[ii]

The basket has been placed among the rushes nearby so it won't get caught in the current. And sure enough, just before mid-day along comes the princess with her maids.

Ruach has already been working, arranging the timing so hormones are right, giving the princess a desire for her own child.

Seeing the basket, she is curious and says to her maid, "Go see what is in that interesting-looking basket."

Soon she can hear a baby crying and when she lifts the cover, she sees him and knows instantly what has happened: a Hebrew mother has followed the edict of her father, only preserving her beloved baby's life, hoping he will be rescued. Then and there she decides to adopt him as her own son.

Miriam watches, forgetting to play, she sees the princess smile at the baby and talk tenderly to him, holding and comforting him. Prompted by Ruach, she runs forward, asking, "Would you like me to get a Hebrew woman to nurse him for you?"

Hatshepsut says, "Yes, do go call one for me," knowing that this must be a sister set up to call the baby's mama. She is glad she can do this for her new baby's mother.

Jochebed is waiting, trying to busy herself; her breathing is praying, yet confident that God is there with her children.

Miriam runs all the way home, so excited and out of breath, she can hardly speak when she gets there. "Mother, Mother! (Gasp!) The princess wants our baby! (Gasp!) She said I should get a nurse! Come Mother!"

Jochebed breathes a relieved *Thank You!* and leaves with Miriam, calming her wildly-beating, joyful heart. *God has great plans for my son! He must have!* "We cannot give away that he is ours," she instructs Miriam. "We will celebrate when we get home if she lets us keep him."

Meanwhile the princess is bathing, excited, and a tinge fearful about what her father will say. *But what can he say! He was in the river and I saved him! I'll call him Moses* (drawn out) *because I drew him out!* The only part that bothers her is *what if he sees it as defiance?* And she decides, *I'll tell him then honestly what I think of his cruel, inhuman law!* (And she must have, because historically it seems the law was repealed soon after it was passed.)[iii]

Just as Hatshepsut is dressed, Miriam arrives with her mother. Jochebed bows and the princess addresses her.

"Thank you for coming to nurse my baby. His name is Moses. Take him and care for him and I will pay you well. I will send my carriage to have you bring him to the palace for visits. Tell me, what is your name? And where do you live?"

Jochebed answers and she and Miriam leave with Moses, controlling their joy and excitement over the success of their experiment, until they are home.

"We get to keep you, baby Moses!" sings Miriam. "Mama, did you hear? His name is Moses!" Three-year-old Aaron's eyes shine, and he sings "Moses, Moses!"

"Yes, my sweethearts, I know. What a nice name for our boy! Can you believe it? Your brother, our baby is Moses, the princess' son!"

"How long will she let us keep him, Mama?" Miriam is in wonder, just old enough at 12 to grasp that things have suddenly changed, and he won't always be with them.

"I don't know, Dear, but we will keep him as long as she lets us. God will work it out."

"God worked this out, didn't He, Mama?"

"He surely did!" laughs Jochebed (whose name means God is glorious)<sup>iv</sup>, and then she laughs again with her daughter, as another rush of joy surges up. "It was God's idea all along! We will teach you all about God, baby Moses, so you don't ever forget Them (Elohim is plural), won't we Miriam?"

"Yes, Mama, we will!"

And that night there is great celebration in the house of Amram and Jochebed that now legitimately houses their baby boy—suddenly a prince!

## A Historical Note

Tanis (renamed Ramses 200 years later) was mostly built by the Hebrews, but when it started was called Avaris by the Hyksos. Joseph likely served under a Hyksos Pharaoh, and as the Egyptians regained power, the Hebrews were "hired" by Thutmose I auspiciously for their "ability." And many families, probably promised new houses, left their shepherd life and moved north to Tanis to work and live. No doubt the foremen had homes among the Egyptians. And others moved there before long.[v]

We don't know if it was two, five or ten years under Thutmose I before the Hebrews became enslaved working without pay, but the transition must have happened gradually with incentives to move from their nomadic life in Goshen.

Also, two hundred of the four hundred years prophesied to Abraham (Genesis 15:13) passed in Canaan before they moved to Egypt, and another hundred in Egypt with great blessing, so their slavery lasted about 100 years through five different Pharaohs.

 Moses and Aaron grow up in Tanis, not far from where the royals prayed and bathed in the Nile.

Chapter 3

# Moses Gets Ready

## Exodus 2:10-15

*God uses Satan's search and destroy plan to educate Moses and develop his gifts, but it's a two-stage process.*

Jochebed takes her position very seriously. She knows Moses is destined for greatness, and though she doesn't know how long she will have him, she determines to give him the best foundation she can so he will want to be God's man.

Even as an infant she talks to him about the Creator God, teaching him, "Elohim is the only true God, and the only Ones who love us and deserve our worship." She knows he will learn about many gods, so she teaches him that Elohim has saved his life and has chosen him for a special work. As he grows, she tells him his choice is all God needs to be with him and protect him, that God is Almighty and has promised Abraham, their ancestor, to take his people to a land of plenty, and make a great nation of them, not only in this world, but in the one to come.

Perhaps the princess mother, Hatshepsut, knew that he would be a better man if he had a stable beginning until he was 12. Or perhaps her heart was soft and one day she graced his humble home and visited it. The love she saw between Moses and his family warmed her heart, and she couldn't fully take him away until then.

Maybe she and Jochebed had discussed it, and she was impressed that Jewish custom recognized boys as men at 12. We don't know, but some believe that he wasn't a child of four or even seven when he went to live at the palace, and was likely 12. But if he was seven, character and personality experts believe that character is laid down by then anyway. And we see that in Moses.

Between his childhood and manhood there isn't much information, but there is enough to allow us to imagine the backstory of how his character developed. Stephen, in the speech that cost his life,

(Acts 7:22-23) refers to Moses as a man approaching 40, well educated in all the wisdom and culture of the Egyptians, and powerful in words and action. How did this happen?

Imagine with me, that Hatshepsut is close to her father, his little princess if you will, (she is his only legitimate child). Her father, though not at first approving of her rescuing this Hebrew baby, doesn't interfere; (commentators guess that Moses and her words are why he repealed his hideous law).

## Moses at the Palace

Thutmose I is soon captivated by this bright, precocious and well-mannered boy. Whenever Moses visits the palace and her father is available, she takes him to visit; and the clear-eyed innocent child asks questions the king can't answer.

He begins to look forward to the visits of the child, and to ask for him when he isn't around. Soon Moses is favored, and blatantly so.

The priests are concerned. They can see that Pharaoh, (Thutmose I) has hopes to make Moses his heir to the throne. So they work hard to push for the marriage of Hatshepsut and her half-brother

34

Thutmose II, clinching his title to the throne. (History makes this backstory easy.[vi])

They are finally successful when Moses is roughly 20, and still very involved in his studies. He is busy studying debate, speaking, persuasion, languages, writing, history, philosophy and most anything else you can imagine that Egypt could offer. He becomes a great military figure, studying war, conquest, and strategy, and his quick mind and amiable personality make him generally a favorite at grandfather's court.

But the priests of Amen (one of their gods) don't trust him. They can see Pharaoh is grooming him to be king. They are his teachers, and are careful to call him Hapmose, which is his full name in Egyptian, meaning "born of the Nile" or "gift of the Nile god," and was only used by the priests or for formal introductions. His family and friends call him Moses, and by this time, he is insisting on using his common name. (A new twist on "Refusing to be called the son of Pharaoh's daughter"? Hebrews 11:24)

His teachers *like* him, but they can't influence his thinking, and it vexes them that they can't control or mold him. His thoughts reveal a much grander scale of thinking and life than they have, or than their religion offers; and they can't out-debate him or put holes in his philosophy. He refutes their theories, and they worry that his strong views on life and religion are not compatible with Egyptian culture. *What in the world will happen if Moses gets on the throne?* They will be out of a job, and that usually means death in their world.

In one such session a teacher who particularly likes him tries to implore him to conform. "Hapmose, you know your grandfather wants you to succeed him when he dies, so why won't you become a priest of our god Amen?"

"Amose, you know I respect you and my other teachers, I just can't respect your religion. You have your goldsmith make a figure of gold, name it Amen and call it your god. You say it takes care of you, and you bow down and worship it. Don't you see how inferior that is to worshiping the God who made the heavens and the earth? You make it, you invest it with authority, but it's still your creation—a lump of gold, it has no eyes to see, no ears to hear. It has no mind to think or care. How can I possibly insult my creator God by bowing down to your creation?"

One of the priests confronts Pharaoh (grandpa), "Hapmose, isn't willing to be initiated into the priesthood, and you know it is against our religion to have a Pharaoh who isn't a priest."

"Well, make him a priest of his own god then," says his grandfather. "Who says our god is better than his?" Thutmose I is old and has mellowed. He often thinks with horror of the circumstances that he created, which brought him Moses, and almost kept him from having Moses as a grandson. And he thunders, "You know he is the best man in the kingdom for this job!" slapping his armrest for emphasis. And with that the priests leave, inwardly fuming.

And while they don't outwardly oppose him to the king, they question his allegiance. But the king has come to love Moses and doesn't want to hear their warnings.

So why isn't Moses married or promised by 40? (Interestingly enough, his Egyptian mother didn't marry until almost 40!) There may have been a special woman, but in Moses mind he is going to have to choose between the throne of Egypt and delivering the people of God. So he guards his affections. While he loves his Egyptian mother and grandfather, he fears he must one day disappoint them, and he never fully gives his heart to them or to an Egyptian woman.

Ruach is always waiting to guide, but Moses is confident and doesn't ask daily. So Ruach and Adonai agree that since the dark side has had so much influence, They will commission angels to attend Moses and impress him that living as God's man, fulfilling his mission, and getting to the next world is a higher calling, and more important, than being a king in this world.

When Thutmose I is dying, he calls for his daughter.

"Hattie," he says, "I'm dying. I can feel it, and I am sorry I allowed the priests to convince me to make you marry your half-brother. I see now, they were afraid of Moses becoming king. Please make sure that when I'm gone, Moses is crowned Pharaoh. I have told them that is what I want. But I don't trust them."

"Yes, father, but what if Moses won't accept it?" she asks.

"Then you are free of your promise." And with that he dies.

Thutmose II becomes king, Moses mother becomes queen, and the priests begin their insinuations about Moses to her husband in private. She, of course, is planning for Moses to take the throne since she and her husband have not had a son.

## A Cosmic Hint?

As it happens, her husband dies after only four years as Pharaoh, and the priests quickly stage a coup to crown his illegitimate son as king, and keep the queen from installing Moses as Pharaoh. Hatshepsut is made vice-regent since the boy is a small child, and she reigns for 22 years.

Her reign is benevolent and peaceful, with an excellent prime minister, Sememenhut, who excelled in commerce and building, but while she has accepted her position, she longs to see Moses succeed her, as any mother would. However, he sees God's hand in these happenings, and becomes more and more consumed with the thought that God wants him to deliver Israel from oppression.

He often talks with her about the evil nature of slavery and his growing belief that God had her save him to lead the Hebrew people back to their own land. She, of course, asks, "Why don't you take the throne and just free them from slavery here? Why do you need to take them away? Just think of all the good you could do for them and us as Pharaoh!"

He decides to go visit his people and see if he can raise a movement to leave peacefully. *Mother is queen. I'm sure I can convince her to let them go, but where? and to do what? Perhaps I should lead them back to Canaan and if we have to fight there, we will. God has promised His people the land, and I am ready to lead them to it.* So he thinks.

## Moses Makes His Move

Moses has been thinking and praying on the stories he has always heard, and he visits his people to encourage them that God will deliver them and take them to their own land. One day he happens upon an Egyptian beating one of the Hebrews under him. Moses walks over but it has no effect on the taskmaster, and Moses is incensed, looking around he sees no one, and in a moment of passionate anger grabs the beating-stick from the Egyptian and kills him.

After the Egyptian dies, he sees no one besides the Hebrew, and he digs a hole and buries the corpse in the sand. He is not sure how to think or feel, but he hopes that if the Hebrew slave says anything, the Hebrews will realize that he is their deliverer— ready to lead them to freedom.

Back at the palace no one seems to know anything, and he feels sure he is safe. *If they knew, what*

40

*would they think? It's a felony to kill an Egyptian.* He knows he is a threat to the young king who hasn't been officially installed, and he also knows advisors who would interpret this as treason, making it reason enough to have him killed.

That night his sleep is fitful, and the next day he decides to go again to the building site and see how they have interpreted his action. As he approaches in his chariot, he sees two Hebrews shouting. As he walks over to them, one hits his opponent.

"Why are you striking your brother? Surely there is a better way to resolve your differences," says Moses as he walks up.

"Who made you our judge?" retorts the offending Israelite, probably out of fear. "You aren't our prince or ruler! Are you going to kill me like you killed the Egyptian yesterday?"

Now Moses knows. *Not only has it been told everywhere, but they aren't thinking that I can lead them to freedom.*

Moses goes to the elders to find out what they know. (They, unknown to him, have had angels tell them that Moses is the one God has chosen to lead them out of Egypt.) The truth is they aren't prepared for freedom—they aren't ready to go. They have heard that he killed an Egyptian and caution Moses to leave.

Moses, now fearful, realizes that if Thutmose III doesn't already know, he will soon, and when he does hear, he will use it to have him killed. He is sure that when the priests hear of it they will call it treason and advise him that Moses is trying to overthrow him. Perhaps if he leaves immediately Thutmose III won't feel any need to react, or use it to harm his mother, since he hasn't officially been installed yet.

He quickly finds his brother Aaron, and says he must leave, to tell his Hebrew family good-by. He returns stealthily to the palace. He quickly tells his mother what happened, "Tell them the truth, and that I have gone to Arabia, and maybe they won't bother to press the issue. But I must leave to travel ahead of the story, because once the outpost sentries have heard, I will have to stay out of sight."

He rides as far and fast as he can. No one suspects anything yet, and they treat him cordially, used to seeing him on official business. He sells his chariot to the first trader in the desert. To the second, he sells his horse, thinking it better to be on foot, having only to find and carry water for himself. *So much for a peaceful exodus!* he thinks, as he lays in the shade of a bush on the shadow side of the mountain, waiting for the cool of night to continue walking.

After Moses leaves, a greatly exaggerated version of the story is told to Thutmose III: that Moses was causing an uprising and killed some Egyptians and wasn't safe to have in Egypt.

Hatshepsut is questioned by him and the priests, and she tells them openly that Moses killed an Egyptian in a fit of rage for mistreating a slave, and has gone to Arabia. They search his house and find it clear that he is gone, and so simply send out notice that anyone seeing Moses should report his location or bring him in for justice.

Shortly after Moses is gone, Thutmose III is formally installed as Pharaoh. The new young Pharaoh's first formal act is to have Hatshepsut and her prime minister deposed (most likely killed) and he has her name removed from all obelisks and public places.[vii]

Moses wanders in the wilderness, trying to stay out of sight, not knowing if an edict for his capture or death has been issued. He berates himself for losing his temper on the Egyptian, and wonders what has happened back at home.

*What will happen to my mother? and to me now? and to the children of Israel in Egypt?*

*God, have I completely messed up Your plan? The Hebrews didn't seem ready to go? Why? And why did I have to lose it? Why didn't they understand I would lead them out? Why didn't you tell them? Are You done with me for killing an Egyptian?*

*Was I supposed to raise an army and fight? Of slaves?*

*Or was my mother right? Should I have listened to her and fought for the throne of Egypt and become a Pharaoh? Is that what You wanted? It didn't seem like it.*

*Why didn't anything work out? Are Egypt's gods stronger than You, as they claim? But how can that be? Why didn't You do something?*

*Why? Why? Where are You?*

Day and night, walking or resting, the thoughts rolled around and around. He little cared where he went. In his mind his life was pretty much over. He had failed at the task God had called him to. Or had God failed him? He wasn't sure.

*Maybe it was all just stories.*

# Chapter 4

# "Now What?"

## Exodus 2:15-20

*God is never in a hurry.*

Moses has to find water, and soon! Fortunately, even though he doesn't feel it, Ruach is leading him, feeling sad for his confusion and pain. God hates it when we are in pain, but They endure it because They know us so well, and know what we need—to best bring about Their plan.

Moses was ready to lead the Israelites out, or so he thought, but God wasn't ready because the Amorites weren't quite ready to lose their protection, and the Israelites weren't motivated to leave Egypt. Life had improved for them since Moses had become a prince, and Hatshepsut ruled.

And God knows Moses isn't ready, he has years of unlearning to do. He has learned many valuable things in Egypt, but not what God is like. His heart needs to be one with God's heart before he can lead Israel out of Egypt without force. He has to be willing to let God do it Their way, and it will take time for him to think like that. He has grown up full of confidence in his military ways.

He has also grown up with the influence of pagan gods and the grandeur people ascribed to them, and even though he didn't believe in them, he couldn't help but be affected by the beliefs around him. His queen mother built the most magnificent temples in Egypt during her reign. [viii] She and everyone around him were steeped in superstition, and had difficulty thinking beyond it.

Whereas, the God he worships has a people who are enslaved. Many contradictions struggle inside of Moses. *Where is this powerful Creator-God of the Israelites? Why didn't They act? And why didn't Israel's God support his attempt to free them? Why didn't his people follow?* Nothing makes sense in his mind!

Also, Moses is used to being obeyed. His every want has been supplied to excess. He had grown entitled to his life and position, expected success,

47

and it had come to him. Even though confronted and questioned by the priests, he had always won. Just as in war, his campaigns had always been successful. Moses had applied himself, and in courtly life he had always been victorious. Even his grandfather had admired him, and had always bent to his will.

And Moses was wise enough, after grandfather died, to work through his mother wherever he needed her influence. Even though his mother's reign was benevolent and peaceful, he knew that the power of evil priests was behind her co-regent. It was, at best, an unstable situation with hostility and traitors lurking.

*So why do their gods have so much power? Why does cruelty seem to flourish against good people?* He wonders.

He knows he has enemies, he isn't naive, but he has grown  up with force as power—might makes right—so it is natural to assume his God is a God who rules by might and power.

*But where is He? Where **were** They? This mighty band of Three? Why didn't They help me? Or, at least, make me know Their will?* He knows favor also—has always been favored. *So why wasn't I*

48

*favored by this God who had supposedly chosen me for a special work?*

The truth is Moses isn't ready. He doesn't know yet how the God of Abraham works, or even what Their goals are. He doesn't realize that this God, his God, is so big, so powerful They can allow evil time to develop and parade its character before the universe, and take another forty years to finish Moses' education. To him, if God is doing anything, it is wasting time, or being capricious.

And so it is, that Ruach leads Moses to the well, the very one Jethro's daughters use to water their sheep every day. This day is no different. As he sits there resting, after drinking his fill, along comes a flock of sheep and behind them a flock of girls.

Moses is intrigued, and as he watches, he engages them in conversation. "Are you all sisters?" His open face and easy manner disarms their fear.

"Yes," answers one, "there are seven of us."

"You mean to say, you don't have even one brother?"

"Not even one. So our father has given us the care of his sheep."

*How extraordinary*, thinks Moses. "And what does your father do while you tend his sheep?" he asks with good humor, clearly curious.

"He shepherds people!" blurts the youngest.

"He does, does he?" chuckles Moses. "And how does he do that?" he plays with her, wondering what she will respond.

"He just takes care of them," she says innocently.

The oldest responds, smiling, "He's a priest."

"Really? I've known lots of priests in Egypt, what god does he work for?"

"The one true God," responds Zipporah, "the maker of heaven and earth."

Moses is surprised and taken back. "Really? What is your father's name?" he asks. He knows the Midianites are descendants of Abraham and Keturah, but also knows most of them worship idols now.

"His name is Reuel, but most people call him Jethro."

Just then other shepherds with many sheep come up and speak roughly to the girls, shewing them away. "You know we water our flocks first!" They

50

yell, and scare the drinking sheep from the trough, pushing their own in.

Moses, stands up. "Wait just a minute! These shepherds have come first and their sheep are drinking, wait your turn!" His voice is commanding like an army general. And though travel-worn, he has the bearing of one—clearly an Egyptian from his dress and headdress.

The shepherds back off, and he pulls up the bucket the girls are working on, pulls up more and finishes watering their flocks.

As they leave he waves to them, and they wave back until they are little dots in the distance, and then he sits down again, hoping a servant comes back to invite him for dinner. He knows he is in Midian country, and he knows enough of Abrahamic customs to know it is a possibility.

At home Jethro is surprised to see them, and asks, "How does it happen you are home so early today?"

"An Egyptian acted like a general and told the other shepherds they had to wait because we were there first." Zipporah informs her father. "He even finished watering our flock."

"Well, where is he? Why didn't you invite him to eat with us? Go quickly back to the well and see if he is still there and invite him home."

Zipporah obediently leaves for the well, and Moses is delighted to see her, but allows her to fulfil her mission.

"Sir, I'm sorry we didn't extend the hospitality of our father to you. Our father insists that because of your kindness you must come and eat with us this evening."

"I would be delighted to accept," Moses responds and stands and walks with her.

"Are you the eldest daughter?" he asks.

"Yes," responds Zipporah.

"And how does it happen that a girl as beautiful as you are, and the oldest, is still under her father's roof?"

"My father only has daughters so he says he needs me to manage his flocks. He says it's good for girls to have an education and 'useful work', but I think he just wants to keep us all with him until he finds husbands he likes. He teases us and says that once he lets me marry, he will have no peace with all the suitors he'll be mobbed with."

Moses smiles, nods agreement, and comments, "You girls do have some rough working conditions to contend with."

"Yes, father wants us to know how to handle ourselves, and stand up to men. With so many of us he thinks we are safe, and he prays for our protection every morning. Plus, he thinks that shepherding work is good for everyone. 'Develops the best in a person,' he always says."

"He sounds like an interesting man," Moses offers, and so begins the first of many conversations between him and Zipporah.

When they reach home, it is a spacious tent, but quite cozy inside. Jethro welcomes him warmly, and thanks him for helping his girls. "You may wonder what a father is thinking allowing his daughters to work under such conditions, but I want them to be strong women who won't let a man mistreat them." He smiles at his daughters, and Moses feels his love for them.

They all eat together out under the trees, and Moses is relaxed, and actually feels happy for the first time in weeks. Once or twice a thought crosses his mind, *what will I say when he asks me what business I am on?*

But by the time the evening meal is finished, with its light conversation, banter and laughter, he has shared a bit of his story, and after the worship led by Jethro, he feels here is a man whom he can trust with his life. He is grateful God brought him to this man's home, a priest of the same God he serves. Already he can think of ten questions he would like to ask him!

And soon he gets his chance. As the girls prepare for bed, Jethro invites Moses to sit with him by the fire and get acquainted. As dark comes on, the evening turns cool.

Chapter 5

# God Provides

## Exodus 2:21

*And so begins the second stage of Moses'
education…*

The fire snaps and hisses as Jethro and Moses sit down on either side, and Moses, who has been dying to talk to Jethro, leans forward and blurts, "Tell me what you know about God! Has He ever spoken to you? How do you know His will? Why does He hide Himself? Why doesn't He act for his people?"

"Whoa!" laughs Jethro, "one at a time!"

Moses at dinner had answered their questions with his story, saying, "When the king decreed that all Hebrew baby boys should be killed, my mother put

55

me in a basket on the Nile, and the princess found me and adopted me. So even though I look Egyptian, sound Egyptian, and was raised Egyptian, I am really a Hebrew."

His listeners had been enthralled, eyes wide, fixed on their guest. Jethro had been both amazed and pleased that God had brought Moses to him. "So why are you here?" he had asked.

"My mother, the queen, and my grandfather, the Pharaoh, wanted me to be king, but I have believed my whole life that God had a special work for me to do—even thinking I was to deliver Israel from Egyptian bondage. But when I tried to lead them, they wouldn't follow. And then the whole operation went south and the king-elect was told I wanted to take his throne, and I knew he would put out an order to kill me and I had to leave. I hoped my leaving would keep my queen-mother safe."

"But isn't she the queen?" had asked one of the girls.

"Yes, but there are powerful men who want to see someone else on the throne instead of her."

"But why not you?" had asked one of the older daughters.

"Because I'm a Hebrew, and I won't worship their Gods." Everyone had fallen silent, looking at Moses in awe. And so Moses had turned the conversation to them and their studies.

Now alone with Moses, Jethro asks, "Tell me what really happened."

The young, strong warrior in front of Jethro leans forward. "I went out and visited the Hebrews and their elders, trying to raise an army to leave in case we were opposed, but they were apathetic. I wanted to lead them out before my mother's reign was challenged by her co-regent—an illegitimate son of her late husband. Why didn't God get them ready? Why did God put it on my heart and not theirs?

He shook his head and continued, "So the last time I went to them, I came upon a master beating a Hebrew worker and, enraged, I killed the Egyptian. No one saw it, and I thought when the Hebrew I defended told how I had rescued him, they would understand I was ready to lead them to their promised land, but they didn't. They turned against me!

"You're God's priest, so tell me. Did I mess it up by killing the Egyptian? Is God angry with me? Have They forsaken me?"

Jethro has been carefully listening, and now asks, "And then the word got to your mother's co-Pharaoh that you had killed an Egyptian?"

"Yes, and I'm sure the priests made it sound like I was trying to take the throne from Thutmose III by insurrection of his slaves. Some of the priests didn't trust me because they couldn't control me."

"Yes, I guess that could get you killed," responded Jethro. "Fear is a great motivator for control. But as to God not motivating them, I can't answer you. I still believe in Elohim like Abraham did, and I see and feel Their might daily, but I have learned not to predict Their behavior. They take Their time. I have heard of the prophecy given Abraham that God would deliver his people from Egypt. You were told you were the deliverer?"

"As far back as I can remember. My father used to tell me that angels had told him. And my mother believed him, especially after my rescue by the princess. She must have told me every day of my childhood that the Creator was the only true God, and the gods of Egypt were no more than what they were made of by the men that made them. And she always said God had a special work for me to do.

"Well, of course, I couldn't take the initiation rites of the priests. They told me my queen mother would disown me if I didn't, that I couldn't be the king unless I went through their initiation and worshipped their gods. So when they staged a coup and put Thutmose III in as king, I thought it was God telling me that They had other plans for me— to lead Israel out. I used to get so angry to see how they were treated—my people!

"Wasn't it natural for me to want to deliver them? But even the elders of Israel told me I should leave; that it wasn't safe. I told them I had led many military campaigns, we would be fine if they would act quickly—my mother was still queen. But they acted so strangely—like they were content to stay."

"That would be hard to understand," agrees Jethro. "I don't have answers for you, I'm afraid you will have to get them from God yourself, but you are welcome to stay with us while you are doing that. As you can see I could certainly use someone to oversee my flocks. You would have work and food and family. I would pay you. You are going to need to earn a living, isn't that true? And there are no better vistas than the faces of my daughters and the mountain peaks of Horeb!" Jethro smiled.

Moses smiled back. "You do have a beautiful family, and your offer is most gracious. I'm just not sure how good of company I will be in my present state of mind."

"You saw how they related to you at dinner! Just don't let your brooding invade our family time. "Keep it for the sheep, herding sheep develops the best in a person, and gives you lots of time to be alone with God. What do you think?"

*Egyptians loathe shepherds, isn't this a fitting exile!* Moses thinks. But he looks Jethro in the eyes and smiles, aware of his blessed fortune in finding this man who so graciously invited him to share his home after only a few hours of knowing him. "Yes, I will accept your kind invitation. Thank you."

"And I think I just might know some people you could talk to that may help you sort things out," offers Jethro. "Perhaps before you settle in here, we could pay Job's kids a visit. They have an amazing story to tell. I'd like to hear it again myself."

**A Timely Visit**

After a couple of days, Moses and Jethro leave on camels for the area North of them, the land around Uz.

That night they camp, and again over a fire, Moses asks, "Why are we going to Edom again?"

"So you can hear Job's story."

"And that is about God?"

"Yes, a story of a righteous man suffering when he had no idea why. His friends came to comfort him and made it worse, ending up opposing him. But God showed up for him. I could tell it to you, but I think you need to hear it for yourself from one of his sons. It has become their vocation, if you will."

"Really? Who was Job?"

"Do you know who Jacob and Esau are?"

"Yes, I think so. It's been a long time since I heard the stories. Abraham's sons?"

"Yes, His grandson's, twin sons of Isaac."

"That's right. We Israelites are descendants of Jacob whose name was changed to Israel."

"Yes. Job was his great-nephew, his brother Esau's great-grandson. A true worshiper of God, who married Jacob's daughter, Dinah. A great and

61

wealthy man." Jethro stretched out and yawned. "Good night, Moses."

"Good night." Moses lay on the ground looking at the stars. *God, my real mother taught me that You are love as well as might. Then why do you allow Your people to suffer?*

And then it was morning, and another day of travel. That night Moses asks what Jethro knows about Abraham, "Would you refresh my mind on the stories my Hebrew mother used to tell me." And Jethro obliged.

The next night Moses asked for more, and he was somewhat comforted by the familiar stories that brought such warm feelings of home.

Then they reached one of Job's sons, now an old man, and told him why they had come. *This must be how Abraham looked* thought Moses. The man fairly glowed as he smiled and embraced them, happy to tell his father's story again. The peace of the old man seemed to surround all of them and hold them, as he told of his father's tremendous blessings and then incredible losses all in one day.[ix] He shared the pain of the disfiguring illness that followed, the visit of his friends that turned out to add to his pain, and finally how God showed up in the storm.

Moses is awed, unaware of the passing of time, caught up in the drama of the characters, *how could these "friends" blame him for his misfortune? And why was this happening?* At one pause he even interrupts. "Did he ever find out?"

The old man smiles. "God did show him, much later in a dream, some councils in heaven, and the challenge that caused the test. But let me save that for last."

Moses thinks he will burst before they reach the end and the stories of the councils in heaven. He is awed at the story. *So God is good and They are opposed!* He could hardly stay sitting! This he had never heard before! *God is involved in a war Themselves!*

He could hardly sleep that night. And the next day he quizzes the old man again, who graciously and patiently answers his questions and repeats parts of the story for Moses. At one point he says, you know, my father always wanted the story to be written, but none of us felt able to do it, outside of a few pictures we wrote down to help us remember the details.

"I've never seen anyone so taken with it as you are. Are you able to write?" And with that he becomes the questioner, asking Moses of his education, ability and background. "Would you be willing to write my father's story?"

Moses feels a thrill pass through him; now he has a purpose, besides answering his own questions and herding sheep. "I would be honored. I will write it and bring it to you to review for accuracy." And they embrace Job's son and leave.

All the first day of travel, Moses' mind is a whirl with connections coming to him from the story as he replays it again and imagines the characters. That night around their fire he asks Jethro to tell it to him again since he'd heard it before, and back and forth together they fill in all the parts.

Finally, on the third night he asks Jethro, "Tell me what you know about our beginning, how did we come to be? Do you know the setting, the conditions surrounding our world when God created us?"

And Jethro begin to tell him everything he knew— all the stories he had heard about God and creation. They talked long into the night, Moses stopping him often to ask questions.

At home again, the stories and their talks continue. Moses is a man obsessed with getting information about God and his dealings with man. And often

Zipporah or another of the girls finds him writing while the sheep graze. He first had to come up with a way to write words that were easier and quicker than hieroglyphs.

True to his word, he made another trip to visit Job's son, months later, and hear the story again. After which, he worked a few days, and then read his account to the old man who smiled with delight when he had heard it!

"Magnificent! My father would be so happy!" was his grateful response. "May we make a copy of it? And return it to you?"

"I've already done that," answers Moses. "I knew I would want one of my own. This is your copy, and this is how the letters make words," and he taught him how to read this language of sounds.

The next morning, the old man bowed to Moses and repeated his gratitude, adding a blessing on Moses as he leaves for his new home at Jethro's.

Chapter 6

# Wasted Time?

## Exodus 2:21-3:1

*God sees things very differently than humans do.*

It wasn't uncommon for Jethro to hear about Moses at dinner, even if he was out miles away with the sheep and staying with them overnight. His daughters were eager to go and see how he was doing and take him food. If he was close by, they asked to go and "help" him. But if he was far away, Zipporah was the one Jethro asked to go, sending along a servant if it was very far. The others often begged to be allowed to accompany her.

Zipporah was happy to have them go with her, but she really enjoyed Moses company, and before long she would slip off without an attendant, letting only her mother know where she was going.

Moses was always glad to see any of them, but he especially liked it when Zipporah came alone, and one day he asked her to come in the morning and he would read to her what he had been writing. It became a regular thing. She loved those times, and realized she was developing feelings for him. Some days they would just talk and he would ask her what she thought about things. She loved feeling so important to him, and soon her mother and father noticed the special bond between them.

All of Jethro's girls loved Moses and he treated them all well, but Zipporah was bright as well as beautiful and she thought for herself. She was deep and solid and he loved her perspective. He opened up to her and shared what it had meant to him to write the story of Job for his family. She was impressed with his ability as a writer and a poet, and told him so.

He also shared his questions about God, and asked her thoughts. He would tell her how being out there alone with the sheep and with God was changing him. He had always been so sure that his ideas and his ways were right, but now he seemed to question everything. He shared how he felt

God's presence, and sometimes felt as if God was speaking to him. At first he had been afraid to think it was God. But then he began to welcome it, and even ask Him questions.

"I used to think the temples and obelisks in Egypt were such amazing works of architecture, and thought surely their gods must have helped them. Even so, my natural mother's words were always in the back of my mind that their gods were really no gods at all. But I had to wonder why the people of those gods prospered, while the people of my God suffered in slavery. It didn't make sense to me why The Almighty's people suffered, while the Egyptians became so powerful and built such magnificent cities.

"Writing Job's story helped me see who our God is. He is so much bigger, so much greater than idols! I had to add what God told Job to the story in a prologue—about why he was tested—so everyone could understand! That helped me so much! What perspective it gave! God must be fighting a war!

"Zip, do you think They wanted me to be Pharaoh?"

"Maybe. You could have done a lot for God as Pharaoh." She smiles shyly, "And this surely isn't as important, but then I wouldn't have met you."

To which Moses responds, "It's important to me! You all have come to feel like my home, but you are the hearth, my rest and reward at the end of the day. And sometimes in the middle of it!" and, smiling, he took her hand.

In a couple of years he asks Jethro if he can marry his oldest daughter, and Jethro is happy to oblige. The wedding is sweet and simple with lots of guests, food and dancing.

After the wedding, Zipporah begins accompanying Moses with the sheep. Now they take their own tent with them and have hours and hours to talk.

"Sweet shepherdess," Moses would say, "Do you think God is more like a warrior or a shepherd?" Or sometimes, "Sweet One, do you think it takes a greater God to build these mountains or to help men build temples?" He is always trying to figure out what God is really like, and what his life means.

**Transformation in Moses**

This transformation is partly engineered by Ruach, who is drawing him more into a shepherd's view of God than a warrior's. Moses already has that side. He knows how to run a campaign and subdue people. In his mind he can even do it humanely. Moses definitely leans toward the mighty view of God. But God delights in freedom and love, and Moses doesn't know Them that way.

He did glimpse it through Job's eyes when writing that story. *Can it be that God loves evil-doers so much that They want them to be as happy as they can be (given their choices) during their short span on earth?* He wonders. *There is definitely more to God than just winning...* Ruach is getting him ready to write Genesis for Them—the book of beginnings.

When the thought to write the stories he has heard from Jethro first comes, he is giddy with excitement, and then overwhelmed by the enormity of the task. *But yet how hard does it need to be?* he thinks. *I don't have to write it like Job's story. It doesn't need to be poetry. I could just write prose. People just have to know how big and how good God is! There just needs to be a record of important events.*

And so it happens, after a day by himself, because Zipporah is pregnant and not feeling well, that he

71

goes home to tell her his new idea. He will write a book about God and the beginning of earth!

Moses is so excited. "Maybe God can't use me as a deliverer, but They can use me as a writer," he tells her. And immediately he begins.

They stay close to Jethro's home whenever they can because soon Gershom is born. The first grandchild! Moses names him "banishment" showing that there is still pain from feeling like he is in exile far from home. Staying close by, gives Moses opportunity to ask Jethro to repeat his stories, and read what he has written for his feedback.

In three more years his second son is born. Moses wants to circumcise him on the eighth day according to Abraham's instructions for keeping God's covenant. Zipporah had grudgingly complied with Gershom, but objects with Eliezer. "Moses he is a tiny baby," she says this time, "and this isn't Israel, and they are half Midianite. Please don't do this." And he gives in to her wishes.

Forty years Moses works for Jethro, who is now an aging priest, and Moses' best friend, though Ruach is vying for that position. And one day in heaven Ruach is discussing timelines with Abba and Adonai.

## The Godhead Confers

"Do you think he's ready yet?" Adonai asks. We are at the end of the time set for the Amorites to decide their allegiance. For the most part they have given themselves to the other side, taking the easy way instead of seeking Us. We can send them a prophet as one last attempt and appeal, but since Thutmose III has died the Israelites are really suffering. Amenhotep II has proved to be a terrorist, out-stripping his father in notoriety for evil. His name will surely go down as a synonym for a devil."

"Then let's act," says Abba. "Is Moses ready, Ruach?"

"I believe he is, now that he doesn't think so." Ruach smiled. "He has become tender and reverent and teachable. Being with sheep, having children, writing, conversing with Me, have all worked together to make him a compassionate but firm leader. He's not so impatient for action now, doesn't insist on his way, has become the most teachable human I know. We might need to convince him that he is our choice!"

"Very good. What is your plan for communicating with him, Adonai?"

"I thought maybe something he can't understand or explain. I'll go as Michael, the Angel of the Lord, and let him see the raw energy of fire that doesn't consume but gives life. He will have to come to Us and investigate, and then I will have the right to speak face to face in a way that he will not doubt. If I go as a human, he will question it.

"That's good." Ruach observes, "He is pretty sure we are done with him except for his writing ability. What do you think about having Aaron go to meet him?"

Ruach always has a soft spot for the weakness of Their humans who lose faith in being disappointed and disillusioned, and who struggle to come back to faith. "I can speak verbally to Aaron and set it up—tell him when to leave and where to go. I'll send another angel to go with him in addition to the one he has. I'm pretty sure he will be responsive."

"Sounds good," says Abba. "I'm ready to deal with Satan's little puppet on Egypt's throne. And I'm glad this will give him one more chance to see power used for good. He's pretty hard, not likely he will turn around, but it will be a great demonstration for the universe and the world."

## Aaron Hears God

And that is how it happens that one night in Egypt, toward morning, a voice calls "Aaron, wake up! I AM the God of your father Abraham, and I AM going to appear to your brother Moses in Midian, where he is herding sheep for Jethro. I AM going to tell him it is time for him to come back and lead Israel out of Egypt. I want you to go meet him. He will have many doubts and objections, but when I guide you to him, he will be encouraged. You can speak for him."

"All right, Lord," answers Aaron, slightly shaken and now fully awake. "When should I leave?"

"In two days. My angels will guide you to the well at Horeb and Moses will be there," Ruach ends.

Aaron wakes his wife to tell her, "God just told me to go meet my brother."

"The one who left years ago?" she asks sleepily. "Are you sure it was God and not a dream?"

"Yes, that's why I woke you, so I wouldn't second guess it, or think I imagined it. I'm taking Nadab. We'll be back in two weeks. You'll be OK."

Then he tells Nadab, who is excited to go.

And in two days they set out.

Chapter 7

# God Makes an Appearance

## Exodus 3:1-4:19

*God loves doing the unexpected.*

Summer is just past, an unusually dry summer, and Moses and his sons are taking the flocks way around to the back side of Sinai, where there is more shade, and an easier way up the mountains. It is harder to keep track of the sheep there, but the grass in the desert has long since dried up. So they have taken them up Horeb, a range of mountains, and through its Wadi and a narrow pass into a large and usually grassy meadow surrounded by high rock walls, each of them watching a third of the flock.[x] Even here the grass is sparse, and they

77

spread out. Moses is at the bottom of a huge granite peak called Sinai.

He is alone, scanning, keeping an eye on all of his sheep when he sees a fire. He has seen fires on the desert in 40 years; as long as you could keep on the right side of them, they cleaned off the dead brush and burned out. But there is no smoke to this one. *That's odd*, he thinks *I should be able to smell it. I'll go check it out.* As he gets closer, he sees that, though engulfed in flames, it's not burning up! *Why this is a wonder!* he marvels, as he walks toward it. *It doesn't seem to be spreading either.* Everything, branches, trunk, and green leaves of the large thorn bush are burning but not being consumed. They are illuminated, looking more verdant than ever.

As in awe he watches, he hears a voice call him.

 "Moses! Moses!"

"I am here," he says in wonder.

"Be careful. Take off your sandals, for the ground where you stand is sanctified by My presence and could ignite you too."

Quickly Moses leans over and slips off his sandals, and the voice continues. "I am the God of your father, and the God of Abraham, Isaac and Jacob."

Moses covers his face with his arm, suddenly afraid to look on God, (This has been happening ever since Jacob was afraid, yet later he wrestled with Him. Is it a guilt thing? Abraham wasn't afraid.)

Adonai, as Michael the Angel of the Lord, [xi] continues. "I have seen the suffering of my people Israel in Egypt, and have heard their cries to Me because of their mistreatment. I know their pain and am ready to deliver them from the Egyptians, to bring them into a large land flowing with milk and honey in place of the Canaanites, Hittites, Amorites, and others. I have heard them groaning under oppression and heard your prayers for them. Come now, and I will send you to Pharaoh, so you may bring My people out of Egypt."

Moses is stunned. Yes, he had prayed for them day and night but he had long ago given up on being their deliverer. He hasn't spoken Egyptian in 40 years! So haltingly he answers, "Who am I? That I should—go to Pharaoh—and bring your people-- Israel out of Egypt?" He's thinking *Thutmose III could still be Pharaoh and I could still be a "wanted" man!*

"I will surely be with you; that will be your sign that it is I who have sent you. Also, when you have brought the people out, you shall all worship Me here on this very Mountain."

"But suppose I go to Israel and say, 'The God of your fathers has sent me to you,' and they ask 'What is His name?' What should I say?"

"I AM who I AM," answers Michael. "You are to say to them, 'I AM has sent me to you. Tell them, 'Adonai, the God of your fathers, Abraham, Isaac, and Jacob has sent me to you.' This is my name forever and the name by which I should be remembered from generation to generation.[xii]

"Go now, gather the elders of Israel together, and say, 'Adonai the God of Abraham has appeared to me saying, I have been paying close attention to my son Israel and have seen what is done to you in Egypt. I promise to bring you out of your affliction into the land of the Canaanites, Hittites, and Amorites, to a land full of grass and flowers where you will always have plenty.'

"They will listen to you. Then you and the elders of Israel will go to Pharaoh and say, 'Adonai, the God of Israel has met with us, and we ask permission to allow us to go three days journey into the wilderness to offer sacrifices and worship our God.'

"But I know Pharaoh, and he will not let you go except by overwhelming him. So I will stretch out My rod in your hand and strike Egypt with all My wonders, and after that, he will let you go. Then I will give Israel favor with the Egyptians, so you will not leave empty-handed. Every woman is to ask her neighbor for silver, gold, jewelry and clothing for the celebration. She will dress her whole family in them, and so they will be properly paid when you leave Egypt."

Moses objects, "They didn't believe me when I was a prince, 40 years ago, and wouldn't follow me then; why should they believe me or listen to me now? They will say 'Adonai has not appeared to you.'"

"What is that in your hand?" asks Michael.

"A shepherd staff," answers Moses.

"Throw it on the ground," says Michael.

Moses throws it down and it becomes a poisonous hissing snake! He jumps back.

Michael directs, "Now pick it up by the tail."

Moses is thinking *you never pick up a snake by its tail!* But since it is God speaking, he steps behind it, reaches out and quickly grabs the tail, and it turns into his staff again. Moses is impressed.

"This is so they will believe that Adonai, the God of Abraham, Isaac and Jacob has sent you. Now put your hand inside your tunic and take it out again."

So Moses put his hand inside and took it out, and it was white with leprosy!

Michael continues, "Put your hand back inside your tunic."

Moses did, and when he took it out it was restored just as it looked before.

"If they don't believe you, or the first sign doesn't convince them I sent you, they will believe the leprosy. But in case they still don't believe you, take water out of the Nile and pour it on the ground while they watch. When it hits the ground it will be blood."

"But Adonai, I am not a ready speaker, you've just seen how I stumble over my words. And I haven't spoken Egyptian in 40 years!"

"Who made your mouth? Or for that matter your ears and your eyes? Who designed man? Is it not I, Adonai? Now go, and I will be with you and teach you what to say."

"Please, Lord, send someone else. Forty years ago I was ready, but now I see that I'm not the man for the job." Now he is past humility. It has gone over into *I'm really afraid You can't qualify me to do the job!* Never mind that it is God promising success.

"Moses!"

*Wow!* Thinks Moses, *He almost sounds angry!*

"Your brother Aaron is coming to meet you as we speak, and I know that he can speak well."

(*Is that humor I hear?* wonders Moses.)

"He will be very glad to see you. You will meet him here."

*It must be for emphasis,* thinks Moses, *He can't be angry and joke at the same time. My brother is on his way here? I guess God isn't asking if I want to. This is the real deal—what I always thought about!*

Adonai continues, "You are to tell him what I tell you and he can speak Egyptian or Hebrew for you. He will be your spokesman and you will be as God speaking to him. And don't forget to take your staff with you." And then He is gone.

*He does have a sense of humor!* thinks Moses. *He knows how rattled I'll be leaving. I think I'll keep this between us for the time being. If I tell Jethro or my wife what God has said they might think I should go alone.* And so thinking, he whistles for his two sons.

"We're going home now," he says, "let's get started. It's going to take us all day to get back." And down the mountain they go, his head in a whirl. *If Aaron has already left Egypt we only have a few days to get home, get ready and get back. We can stop here until he meets us.*

To his sons he says, "I've decided to take you on an adventure. We are going to go visit my family in Egypt!"

The two young men (between 25 and 35) look at each other with expressions of incredulity and excitement. *Where did this come from?* But they are definitely ready for an adventure! On the way home, Moses worries about leaving Jethro with his flocks. *Maybe one of the girls' husbands or sons can take over for me—I'll suggest it, I don't want to put him in a bind.*

Time is of the essence, and when they arrive long after dinner, Moses goes straight to Jethro, saying, "I don't want to put you in a bad spot, but this morning, on the mountain, I decided that I want to go and see my family in Egypt, and see if any of them are still alive. Will you be ok with that?

Maybe one of your sons-in-law or older grandsons can keep the sheep?"

"Do you think it will be safe by now?" asks Jethro.

"God has put it on my heart, so I hope so."

"Certainly, go! When are you planning to leave?" Jethro looks at him closely, wondering what has happened, and why he isn't sharing it.

"I want to take my family with me—introduce them. So as soon as Zipporah can be ready—a day or two?"

"It's OK. Go in peace," answers Jethro, thinking *something looks different about him.*

That night, Moses, true to his melancholy temperament, starts worrying about taking his family. *What if Thutmose III is still king and decides to mess with me? God didn't say take your family. Should I leave them here? I'd never forgive myself if something happened to them.* He tosses and turns.

And then he hears a now familiar voice, it's Adonai, "Don't be afraid to go to Egypt, Moses. All those who sought your life are dead."

Relief floods him, and there in the dark he whispers, "Thank You, Adonai, thank You!" and falls asleep.

Chapter 8

# Surprises along the Way

## Exodus 4:20-28

*Understanding the Covenant may take more information.*

Moses tried not to sound demanding, as he asked his family to get ready to leave. Zipporah had been shocked at this sudden turn of events, and quizzical. He had shared with her that God had appeared to him and told him to go home, but he didn't tell her anything else, except that God had said Aaron was coming to meet them. The time to explain was not right—she might get worried. He had seen questions in her eyes as it was.

Now she asks, "Are you excited? Should we be scared?"

He is glad he can tell her he couldn't sleep that first night for worrying if he should take his family, and how Adonai had spoken into his fears that those who wanted to kill him are dead. He can see it brings relief to her too.

There will be plenty of time to tell her and the boys the rest of his story on the way. He wonders how much Aaron knows, *had Adonai told him what was going on? Why does Aaron think he is meeting me? If Adonai is leading him he will make good time. We should get going.*

And so on the third day, they eat and kiss all of Jethro's family goodbye and leave on donkeys after the heat of the day, giving them just enough time to get half-way to Horeb. They camp long after sunset.

The full moon makes it easy to set up a tent and roll out bedrolls, his sons helping while his wife sets out a light meal. Later, after his family sleeps, Moses walks around outside, sitting on a rock, getting up again and pacing. *How should I tell them?* he wonders? Now that he has accepted the assignment he has put his whole heart into it, and wants to get it right. The fact that he feels his weakness shows that he understands his need to depend on God—this is the best evidence God can trust him (or us).

*Should I tell them before we meet Aaron or wait till afterward? Should I tell them everything God said? Everything that happened?*

*Will Zipporah feel tricked if I don't tell her before she hears it with Aaron? I've shared so much with her about my questions and doubts. I'd better tell her tomorrow before we meet Aaron. She will feel better about that. She will want to hear it twice anyway. I hope she believes me. It sounds so crazy; God help her believe me! And while you're at it, help Aaron, the Israelites and Pharaoh believe me!*

Adonai has stayed close, and again Moses hears the voice that he has come to know. "Moses, when you go to Egypt, you will do all the wonders I have put in your hand. I'm glad to see you remembered your staff. It is the rod of God now.

"But you need to know, the very presence of My power will cause resistance and harden Pharaoh, and he will not let them go. Then this is what you will say to him, 'Adonai says, 'Israel is My firstborn son, I have asked you to allow him to go serve me, but you refused to let him go, so I will refuse to protect your firstborn from the

Destroyer.'[xiii] After that happens he will let you go." And once again, with that assurance, peace comes, and Moses can sleep.

## Moses Tells Zipporah

The next day Moses walks beside Zipporah's donkey and shares with her "the rest of the story." She is amazed. "You saw God, Moses? And He told you to go and deliver your people?"

"I saw fire and heard His voice."

"Moses, this is what you always believed you would do! It's happening! How do you feel? Aren't you excited? I can't believe you didn't tell me!" Then she grows serious and he sees fear and doubt take over the excitement she feels for him. "Are you going to be a general and lead an army?"

"That is why I didn't tell you. I don't exactly know. And I was afraid you might not want to come if you knew the reason we are going. I was afraid your father would want you and the boys to stay there, and I wanted my family with me. Are you upset with me? Are you afraid to go?" Moses asks.

"Well-l-l," she draws it out, "not really afraid. Do you think there will be fighting—as in battles? That's what you thought originally. You were going to lead them in war. Remember, I used to tease you about your desire to fight and told you I didn't want a bloody bridegroom."

"It doesn't sound like there will be war. God said He will use signs, as I said, and at first Pharaoh will resist, but then he will let us go."

"Will you show Aaron the signs that God showed you?"

"Only if he asks and God impresses me to show him."

"This *is* amazing after 40 years! Maybe God wanted you to be a father first!" she says, and then they both say together laughing, "and herd sheep because it brings out the best in a person!"

"Do you think it is has?" he asks.

She looks at him to see if he is joking, and seeing he is serious, she says, "Absolutely! You were all about war in the beginning, and don't hate me for this, but a lot about yourself too. You are much more attentive to others needs now," she smiles and he smiles back, remembering that frustrated, anxiety-ridden, know-it-all young prince who was running for his life and came to their well.

"It's hard to give up your throne and then have your life's work stripped away too. Especially, when you think you may be the reason!"

"I know." She responds, "But you have come a long way, My Love."

"Thank you. I hope Adonai thinks so."

"He obviously thinks you're ready to lead your people now."

"Life is so ironic, isn't it?" Moses muses. "I thought God had me raised a prince so I could learn military strategy and how to run a campaign and defeat an enemy; that's why I excelled in it. And He probably doesn't care about that at all."

"I am so glad!" she says it playfully in mock relief. I wouldn't want to be married to a bloody general."

He grins and she goes on, "But look at what you did get: all that education in languages and cultures and people!"

"**And writing!**" they both say at the same time, and laugh again.

"I would never have imagined I would end up a writer!" he shakes his head. "That was probably God's way of getting my doubts about Them and suffering straightened out—mostly my picture of God's faithfulness and ability—Their strength. I suppose that is pretty important to leading Their people."

"Yes, more important than knowing how to fight!" she assumes a superior look to enhance being right.

He nods, grinning, relieved that her fear seems gone, "Speaking of importance, I need to tell you something that has come to mind, so that if it should come up, you will be prepared." She looks at him purposefully as he continues, "It may become an issue that we didn't circumcise Eliezer when he was a baby."

"**Why?**" she asked it with emphasis.

"Remember I told you it is the sign of the covenant God made with Abraham. We were just talking about what would be important in a leader. I'm guessing the sign of His covenant in their bodies may be important."

"Ugh!" she responds, "it's like marking your territory."

"Yeah, maybe so, but it's better than burning an X on their foreheads, or even their hands, branding them."

"I would think it would be more important just to have them marked in their hearts," she observes, "as in believing or swearing an oath of faithfulness or something."

"I think that is what Job's story shows," he thinks aloud, "what you believe about God and having a relationship with Them is the most important marker. This must be some sort of special symbol that They use to mark the children of Abraham since God chose his family to send Messiah through. Maybe it has significance for the war They're in."

"Well according to what you have said, it certainly hasn't kept them from suffering!"

"I know, I was just thinking the same thing. But, you know, it might have something to do with requiring permission before God's enemies can touch them, as with Job. Perhaps it protects boys—and fathers--with the 'sign' carved in them. Would that make you feel better about it?" he smiles at her.

"I don't think anything would make me feel good about it. But yes, that would make me feel better."

"Good, let's stop and eat and rest. It's almost midday and it looks like we are getting close to our turn up the mountain."

"Why are we going up there?"

"Adonai said I should meet Aaron there. So I marked the spot. You will get to see the spot where I saw God.

"Did you really see Him?" Zipporah asks in awe.

"I saw fire—remember the thorn bush on fire but not burning—it actually looked better after the glory of God!" he remembers, his face full of wonder.

Moses decides they will stop at a well that marks the end of grazing territory. Many shepherds didn't go up the mountain.

**Another Surprise**

As they approach the well, a shining being with wings approaches Moses, grabbing him in a neck hold, his other hand holding a knife at his throat.

Zipporah is terrified, instantly recognizing the situation as what Moses has just warned her about. She shouts to Eliezer ahead of them, to come at once, and she slides off the donkey and finds a stone knife in the saddle bag. Eliezer rides up and looks terrified at the sight of the angel and his father. Gershom, right behind him, has the same expression.

"This is because I wouldn't let your father circumcise you when you were an infant. You don't have the sign of the covenant that God made with Abraham which marks you as His and protects you, so we are going to have to do it now.

The young man looks like he feels sick, he knows the difference between him and his brother, and there is no resistance.

"Lay down here," his mother directs. "I guess I should apologize to you. It's my fault we have to do this now," and she cuts off his foreskin just as she had watched Moses do with Gershom years earlier. Zipporah picks up the bloody foreskin and throws it on Moses feet. "You are a bloody bridegroom after all!" she says it with anger.

Fortunately, they had brought along some medicinal herbs that would help with pain and speed healing. She sprinkles the powdered herb on, and then to ease her own nausea, puts some under her tongue.

Then the angel lets Moses go and is gone.

Moses, relieved it is over, sets up camp, glad he has something to occupy him while Zipporah gets over her disgust with the whole operation. *I'm so glad I told her about it,* he thinks as he pitches the tent with his son Gershom.

"What was that about, Dad?" he asks. "Was that an angel? And why did he want to kill you?"

"It was Adonai disguised as an angel, and He didn't want to kill me. He just wanted to make sure I knew how important it was to have both of my sons protected. You were circumcised as an infant, but I let your mother talk me out of circumcising your brother, because I thought God had decided not to use me as the leader of Israel. God had asked Abraham to have all of his males circumcised as a special sign of His covenant with them. I've been learning about the war God is fighting in the universe, and I think this must be a sign that allows Them to protect you because your parents have chosen for you to belong to Them— you are protected by their covenant."

"I'm glad you did it for me when I was a baby!" Gershom exclaims with feeling.

"Yes, done on the eighth day as God directed seems to make it pretty humane."

**A Forty Year Reunion**

As they rest in the shade of their tent, Moses tells his sons about his experience on the mountain and what Adonai has asked him to do. They are excited.

Suddenly, it occurs to him that Aaron could be up the mountain waiting for them. *After the heat of midday passes, I'll climb the mountain* he tells himself. Then in the distance, they see two men approaching.

*Could this be Aaron?* Moses wonders and gets up to meet him. It is! And what a reunion they have! Hugging, kissing and crying! They haven't spoken in 40 years!

"I was just getting ready to go up the mountain. I didn't know for sure where I'd meet you but figured God could get you to that spot if He wanted to."

Aaron laughs, "He told me to meet you at Mt. Horeb, at the well, so I thought to make it before it gets too hot, and here you are! And this is my son Nadab."

Moses hugs his nephew briefly and says, "Come meet my family!" as he turns to take them to his camp and introduce them. Aaron's arrival definitely helps to lighten the mood, and they decide to rest until morning and then walk up the mountain to "the spot" where God had spoken.

Early next morning, Moses, Aaron, Nadab and Gershom climb the mountain. Zipporah isn't as excited about seeing the sacred spot as she had been, and doesn't really care to go. She wants to stay with recovering Eliezer at the camp.

On the way up, Moses explains to Aaron what had happened just as they had arrived at the well yesterday, and how it had affected his wife.

"Poor Eliezer!" responds Aaron, "but I'm glad you took care of that now. It wouldn't have taken long before one of his cousins noticed and told the others and it would have spread through Israel— 'Our leader didn't circumcise his son!' You know how people are. We can wait here a few days for him to recover. I'm sure he isn't the only one that will happen to. Do you know what the plan is?"

"Only what I told you. And Aaron, how did God get you to come?" asks Moses.

"He woke me one night and told me he was calling you back to lead His people out of Egypt, but you would be skeptical. He said you would need me to come and meet you, so I came. He told me what route to take and when to leave. And you were here just as He said." They both shake their heads in wonder.

"I guess we can trust Him," says Moses.

"Yep!" says Aaron. "Man! it is so good to see you!"

When they reach the wide, flat valley surrounded by walls, they see a bush that looks exceptionally better than all those around it, Moses says, "This is it! This is the thorn bush that was on fire but not burning! It was an amazing thing to see! I was about here when I saw the bush burning but not burning up, so I walked over to look at it and heard someone calling my name. That was weird! When I answered, the voice in the fire said He was Adonai and He was ready to deliver His people from Egypt and wanted me to lead them out. I told him He should send someone else, I am not fluent anymore. That's when He told me you were already on your way here, and you would be my interpreter."

"Tell me everything He said, just like it happened!" said Aaron. And Moses did, including showing the signs which happened just as they had for him.

"This is amazing," says Aaron. "All my life I heard you would deliver Israel, little brother; and it's here! Finally! God knows we need it!"

And they sat and talked at the sacred spot for a long time.

Chapter 9

# Going Home

## Exodus 4:29-6:30

*The same sun that melts butter hardens clay.*

Egypt still seems like home to Moses, and as they get closer, Moses' heart beats faster. *I didn't think I would ever come back to Tanis again,* he thinks. *God's ways are so amazing!*

Since they were instructed to go to the elders first, they took Moses' family to stay with Aaron's family, introduced everyone, and after resting and eating, leave to gather the elders.

Some of the old ones remain, and some of them are new, but the main difference is they are all ready to listen and respond. Aaron speaks and shows the signs God had given Moses for them.

103

Now they are ready, saying, "How soon do we leave?"

Moses and Aaron ask the elders to proclaim a Sabbath celebration when everyone will worship God and rest. They are to gather all the people into one grand assembly to hear God's words to them through Moses and Aaron.

There is an elder for each of Jacob's sons and the word spreads quickly through their extended families. The people are moved to hear that God has seen their pain and has sent Moses to lead them out to their own land and freedom.

On Sabbath, Moses tells them how Adonai appeared to him and said that He wants to give them their own land covered in grass and flowers. It sounds like heaven to them in their harsh servitude under Amenhotep II.

Of course there are always skeptics who say, "How do we know this is from God?" But when they see the signs given Moses, they are awed, they believe, and bow in worship. Then music and dancing breaks into celebrating deliverance.

They are asked to stay home from work the rest of the day to celebrate their first corporal Shabbat in many years. Civil disobedience!

"We will talk to Pharaoh," say Moses and Aaron, and leave for the palace. As Moses walks onto the familiar grounds, not a lot has changed in 40 years. The kings court and palace has a very familiar feeling. But instead of feeling the awe he used to feel, Moses feels gratitude that God has allowed him his peaceful life with the sheep, getting to know Him, and true power.

*What would my life have been like if I had stayed here and taken the throne? he wonders. I would likely be dead, by now, by an assassin. Or maybe I would have forgotten God and gotten even more into myself than I was, thinking I was the power that ran the world. I would never have learned what I have. I would never have known Your tenderness and power, Adonai.*

## The First Confrontation

That they get an audience with the king shows Moses knows how the courts of the Pharaohs' work. It was not something a commoner could do.

As already mentioned, Amenhotep II was a terrorist, who coming home from one campaign had hung six captured princes upside-down on his ship just to let others know who he was.

105

This is the Pharaoh in power (son of Thutmose III—vice-regent of Hatshepsut, Moses' queen mother) who Moses addresses through Aaron on that first Sabbath afternoon, "We have been visited by our God, Adonai, who has asked us to gather our people and take three days journey into the wilderness to hold a feast and worship Him."

"Who is Adonai that I should listen to him?" asks Pharaoh. "I don't know him and I will not let Israel go."

"Adonai is the God of the Hebrews, and He says, 'Let My people go three days into the wilderness to offer sacrifices and worship Me,' and if you don't He may strike us with disease or the sword."

(This makes sense since the Egyptians held sacred some of the animals the Israelites would be sacrificing.) They are polite, not even threatening him yet. They make it sound as if their God is like the Egyptian gods and might pour out wrath on his subjects for non-compliance, thus soliciting his cooperation so he won't lose his workers.

The king retorts, "Who gave you, Moses and Aaron, the right to cancel my whole work force?" He immediately goes back to authority. "I hear you gave them today off to rest! Tell them to get back to work!" He isn't too concerned about this God who hadn't rescued his people from servitude to his father, grandfather, or great-grandfather.

He dismisses Moses and Aaron and calls his slave masters, "You aren't to give the Hebrews any more straw for brickmaking, but require the same number of bricks per day. They don't have enough to do, that's why they want to go and sacrifice to their God! They are lazy! That will keep them from listening to this religious nonsense!"

The masters and Hebrew foremen tell the people Sunday morning, "Pharaoh says you have to find your own straw—it will no longer be supplied. But your daily quota of bricks will be the same."

So the people have to glean straw from fields all over the country, and it is impossible to keep up. (The straw caused a chemical reaction that made the bricks stronger.) The taskmasters beat the Hebrew foremen for missing their quota on Sunday and Monday.

So the Hebrew foremen, thinking it's their taskmasters who are angry that they didn't come to work, went together to the king to complain, "Why are you dealing like this with us, your servants? Your taskmasters aren't giving us straw, yet requiring the same number of bricks, and look they beat us because we couldn't make quota." And

107

they showed him their feet. (The custom was to beat foremen on their feet—a very painful and sometimes lethal punishment.) "We could barely come here, but we can't possibly do what they are asking! The fault is theirs, not ours!"

"You are lazy!" shouts Pharaoh at the foremen. "That is why you want to go make sacrifice to your God. Get back to work! No straw will be given and you will be required to produce the same number of bricks!" *This will squash their plans*, he thinks.

## Discouragement

Satan saw his opportunity to discourage Israel from thinking they could leave, and to discourage Moses from thinking they would follow! Did the foremen really think Pharaoh would be reasonable?

Moses and Aaron hear about their visit and are waiting for them outside the palace. The foremen come right to them, "May Adonai judge you because you have made us stink to Pharaoh and his servants!" says one.

"You might as well have given them a sword to kill us!" says another."

Moses and Aaron are silent as they see the pain and discouragement of the foremen. They don't even speak on the way to Aaron's house.

Moses tells Zipporah what happened, and then walks outside alone and sits under a tree, "Adonai, why have you brought evil on these people? Is *this* why you sent me? Ever since I spoke to Pharaoh he has made their life unbearable, and You have not delivered them at all. This is why I said to you 'Send someone else.'"

"Now you will see what I am going to do to Pharaoh," Adonai answers. Notice, He doesn't explain, but directs Moses to the outcome and who He is. "By a strong hand he will let them go—even driving them out!

"I Am Adonai, the very One who appeared to Abraham, Isaac and Jacob as El Shaddai (God Almighty). Yet they knew Me as Adonai, just as you do, and I revealed myself to them as I have to you. I also made a covenant with them to give them the land of Canaan where they were foreigners.[xiv]

"Furthermore, I hear the cries of my son Israel whom the Egyptians are attempting to keep in bondage, and I remember my covenant. Therefore, say to my son Israel: I am Adonai, and I will bring

109

you out from bondage. I will redeem you with My mighty arm and great judgments.

"I will take you for My people, and I will be your God. You will know that I am Adonai your God, who brought you out from under the oppression of the Egyptians.

"So will I bring you into the land I swore to give Abraham, Isaac and Jacob. I will give it to you as an inheritance. I Am Adonai."

Moses tells Zipporah what God said, and then reading her sad eyes says, "I know it's hard on you to see me like this; and Adonai sounds like it's going to get bad here. Would you like to have the boys take you home?"

"Without you?" now her eyes show questions and fear.

"You would be alright with them. They are men and they know the way. I'll prep them, and you could make it before the rain and cold nights start. You could be home in a week. Think about it; I'll talk to them." He mentions it to his boys who are disappointed to miss the action—he'll give them time to think.

Then he goes to Aaron "Have the elders call the people again, and say, 'The God of Abraham,

Adonai, just now told Moses He will bring you out of Egypt according to His covenant with Abraham, with a mighty arm and incredible judgments.'"

Aaron does say it, but the people won't listen because their spirits are broken.

"He hasn't done anything yet!" they say. "We'll believe it when we see it."

Adonai came to Moses right after their assembly and said, "It's time to go speak to Pharaoh, king of Egypt, so he will let my son Israel go out of his land."

Moses is discouraged too, and he answers, "Your "son" Israel has not listened to me so why would Pharaoh?" He is thinking it's his failure, and in effect says to God, *I told you this would happen.*

That evening Aaron and Moses are talking and Moses gets the idea to write a record of everyone in his family who is in Egypt—all the sons of Amram. He asks Aaron to tell him all their names. They decide to start with all the sons of Jacob. But when he gets to Levi they get side-tracked and go down through who married whom and their children.

God knew he needed a break, and this was a good distraction from all the discouragement. Some of these people he remembers, and some are vague recollections, and many came after he was living in the palace.

Talking about the old days and telling their children and wives stories and memories that he and Aaron share, changes the mood and at least takes them back 75 years and then upwards through all the memories of believing he was Israel's deliverer.

That night before he falls asleep, his thoughts clear; *my dream has finally come true!* Zipporah's voice interrupts his thoughts, "If you think it would be better, the boys and I will go home."

"Thank you, My Love. I would feel better, and you will be alright. I think Adonai gave me the idea so I wouldn't be concerned for you, and so you wouldn't have to go through this. He will keep you and the boys safe." He hopes to feel as confident as he sounds.

"I'll send a messenger when we get close to the mountains where God said we would worship Him, and you can come and meet us there. Your father can come too and visit if he'd like."

He wraps his arms around her and prays silently, *I hope I am doing the right thing here.* Once again peace comes and they sleep.

Chapter 10

# The Spiritual Battle Intensifies

## Exodus 7:1-8:19

*God doesn't mind taking the long route; but we do.*

The next morning Moses gets his family ready to leave and goes with them to the outskirts of Tanis, "You can go back, Dad," say his sons. "We'll be fine." They are disappointed, but have also experienced the negativity generated against their dad and them. They are eager for this adventure and ready to go home too.

"Thank you for doing this for me. Take care of your mother." He smiles at them, knowing they would like to stay but are proud he trusts them

115

with the responsibility of taking their mother home. "Remember everything I told you, and don't forget to fill your water skins before you get to the bitter springs, or you will get dehydrated before the next fresh ones." He hugs them all and watches as they ride off on their donkeys until they are specks on the road. "Take care of them Adonai!" he prays. "When will I see them again?"

And Adonai says, "I've got them. Remember that you work for Me—the Creator of the universe. Amenhotep is just a Pharaoh—just a king. You need not feel dejected. I have set you up as God to him, and Aaron will be your prophet. You are to speak everything I command you, and Aaron will translate to Pharaoh. By the time I get done, he will let my son Israel go.

"But you need to know, it isn't going to be immediate, or even quick. As I told you My commands will get his back up, My presence will harden his heart, and I will use that to multiply signs and wonders in Egypt. You haven't even shown him one sign yet!

"He will explain them away, so there will be more and more until everyone in Egypt knows the name Adonai, because of all the phenomena that will happen to them. I will bring my armies out of

Egypt but it will be done My way. They can't fight, but I will fight for them and subdue Pharaoh."

So Moses at 80, and Aaron at 83, go to Pharaoh to command that he let Israel go. And on the way, God says to Moses, "When Pharaoh says 'Who are you that I should listen? Prove yourselves with a miracle,' then you say to 'Aaron throw down the rod of God so it may become a serpent.'"

They go in to Pharaoh and it goes down exactly as God said it would. And when Aaron threw down the staff it became a poisonous snake. Pharaoh is sure this is just magic, and the Egyptians are good at magic, so he calls his magicians and says, "Turn your walking sticks into snakes for these men." And they do!

But then something strange happens. Aaron's serpent eats all of their serpents which weren't really serpents at all. Satan could help them turn their rods into fake snakes, but he couldn't make them real snakes. So Aaron picks up his snake by the tail and it is his staff again! Theirs are gone! Pretty convincing. But Pharaoh blows it off. "So your magic is a little better than ours. They still aren't going! Leave me!"

That night Adonai says to Moses, "Pharaoh is very stubborn, so I want you to meet him in the morning where he goes out to pray to his Nile god. As he comes out of the water meet him on the riverbank and tell Aaron to say, "Adonai, God of the Hebrews has sent me to you saying, 'Let my people go to serve Me, but you have not listened, and so that you will know I am Adonai, the Creator, I will strike the waters in the river and they will become blood and all the fish will die and the river will stink and your people will hate to drink the water of the Nile.'"

Moses and Aaron walk to the Nile at sunrise and deliver Adonai's message to Pharaoh. Then Moses nods to Aaron, and commands, "Take the rod and stretch it out over the Nile, their streams, their pools, their ponds, so that they will all become blood, even in their vessels of wood and stone."

Aaron strikes the water in front of Pharaoh, and suddenly Amenhotep is standing knee-deep in blood! It looks like blood, smells like blood, feels like blood, and soon dead fish come belly-up to the surface while he is calling for his magicians.

"Dig out some water over there and turn it into blood for these jokers," he says.

A few yards away they dig and find water and with their magic arts turn it into "blood." At least it looks like blood, and that is good enough for Pharaoh. He turns and walks away to his palace, dismissing them.

"Good thing Adonai told me it wouldn't be enough, that he is a stubborn man," says Moses to Aaron as they walk home. "I'm glad I sent my family home. This may take a while."

"We should have told his sorcerers to turn the blood back into water!" quips Aaron.

It took seven days before the Nile ran clear again. Meanwhile the Egyptians had to dig wells for water to drink or cook with, and they were upset. The water they found was bitter and salty from the nitrous earth, and they complained.[xv] *How could this happen to our Nile god?*

Moses and Aaron go south to Goshen to see if it is affected. Their wells have water as always. Moses and Aaron share God's message of deliverance with the people there, and prepare them to participate.

After the week of blood has passed, Adonai speaks to Moses, "Go to Pharaoh and tell him, "This is what Adonai says, 'Let My people go, so they may serve Me. And if you refuse, I will strike all your territory with frogs (another of their gods.) Not only the river will swarm with frogs, they will be everywhere with you and all your people, even in your beds and your cooks' bread bowls.' Tell Aaron, 'stretch out the staff over the river and cause frogs to come up over the land'."

They go with their message out to meet Amenhotep at the river as the sun is rising again. He is getting irritated with them but is still unrelenting. They deliver their message and he waves his hand blowing them off.

So Aaron stretches out his rod over the Nile just as before, and suddenly, frogs are hopping out of the water everywhere. In minutes his magicians are beside him and make it look like they bring frogs too. Though with so many how can they tell whose frogs are whose? Pharaoh walks away again, trying hard to appear nonchalant.

Before long he is saying to his magicians, "Take these things away!" It is hard for him to say because one of their gods (Heqa, a goddess) has a frog's head.[xvi] But his sorcerers can't take them away. And in just one day everyone all over is crying out about getting rid of the frogs—gods or not!

The next day he calls for Moses and Aaron. When they arrive he acquiesces, "Ask Adonai to take away the frogs from me and my people, and I will let your people go sacrifice to Him."

Moses responds graciously, "I will even give you the honor of setting the time when you want me to pray and ask Adonai to remove them."

"Tomorrow morning at sunrise," answers the king, hoping they will die or go back in the river before then.

"So be it," says Moses, tomorrow at sunrise the frogs will leave your houses, and only live in the river so that you know there is no one like our God." And he and Aaron leave.

"Do you think he really will?" asks Aaron.

"Take them away? I don't know, I think He will just to show that He's in charge of creation. That's why I made a specific time."

"No, I meant do you think Pharaoh will let us go?"

"Oh, I doubt it. God said he would get stubborn. Once he's comfortable again, he'll think he's back in control."

Early the next morning Moses calls to God, "Adonai, please take away the frogs so Amenhotep and all the Egyptians will know you are in charge of even frogs here."

And God did what Moses asked. Everywhere frogs were dying at sunrise. They raked together heaps of them and the whole country smelled putrid as they decomposed. God could have sent all the frogs into the river or turned them into dust, but then Pharaoh and the people would have thought it was just superior magic, so he let them deal with the natural result of real dead frogs. They burned the great heaps which produced an even worse smell.

But as God predicted, once Pharaoh got relief, he changed his mind, and wouldn't let them go. He sent Moses a message that said, "Your people aren't going anywhere—I am their king."

The resistance is hardening Pharaoh. We are made so that every action creates a pathway in our brain, and every repeated choice or action strengthens that path. Our resistance hardens our hearts against God. So here Amenhotep is in a power struggle with God. Poor stupid man—he doesn't believe the Hebrew's God is the Creator God. He thinks he can win, and he can—for himself and his fate— God is very protective of personal freedom. But he can't rule against God's wishes for Their people—when the time is right, God's plan will prevail.

So God says, "Moses, don't be discouraged it is as I said it would be. Tell Aaron to stretch out your rod and strike the dust with it and the dust will become gnats everywhere in Egypt."

This time God does it a little differently. They don't go do it in front of Pharaoh, God lets him hear it from his own people. And swarms of gnats rise from the ground. But when the magicians of Pharaoh try to produce gnats they can't, and they say to Pharaoh, "This is the finger of God."

But Pharaoh doesn't care, he says, "They probably came from the dead frogs."

The gnats in some versions are called lice. Most translators go with gnats because it is closer to the Hebrew word used. But some think it was lice, and that could be, since Egyptians were known to shave their heads and wear wigs because lice was such a problem.

I can't imagine stinging gnats wouldn't have brought Pharaoh to his knees in surrender again, because the next one does. Lice may have been sort of routine, just a lot more of it. So it could have been lice, and probably lasted seven days like the blood did, because Pharaoh didn't relent and didn't ask for intervention.

Chapter 11

# Lord of the Flies

## Exodus 8:20-24

*Does God destroy?*

*Or does he let the Destroyer do his thing?*

Can Satan create? Normally the answer is "No!" But that brings up an interesting question. Does God create destructive elements—in this case flies? Egypt has historically had the dog fly. It is large and venomous with a painful bite. Where did it come from?

With this plague God instructs Moses to tell Pharaoh, "Flies will not come on the Hebrews because Adonai is making a distinction between Egypt and His special people."

It's possible the first three hadn't affected them either, but this is the first time God specifically tells Pharaoh it won't, to make sure he is aware of it. Does God protect from destruction by Their enemy? As in the tenth plague? Or is it God doing the destroying?

Back to the original question: it is true Satan doesn't have ability to create life from nothing. But we have all seen how he can twist God's gifts and create aberrations. Look at the suffering and disease he has caused with sex—one of God's best gifts. Or the diseases he has created from ignorance of health, of food, of sanitation. Remember in this series how Lucifer was given the chance to study the laws of nature and see what he could create? No doubt, he learned a lot about nature and its laws.

At that time, he was still under God's influence, fulfilling his dream

He had not yet chosen to activate the law of sin and death. But imagine what he must have done in the lab after he had activated entropy. He is called "the destroyer" in Exodus 12:23 and also in the book of Hebrews (2:14). He would destroy all of us (or have us destroy each other) if God allowed. It's who he has become.[xvii]

126

This is the first plague where it says the land was corrupted—literally the Hebrew is "the land was destroyed." Would God have done this? Or would he have allowed the dark side to do their thing? I think it is the latter. I believe God is not the creator of evil or destruction.

Yes, They allow entropy [xviii] to exist for choices, but They are winning the "right" **now** to banish evil, keeping it only as a personal choice forever, because it brings death. God has allowed Satan to have the power of death as long as he is kept alive. When God stops shielding him, he and all of his will cease to exist. (Isaiah 33:1)

There will be no more death or destruction. Revelation 20 says even death and hell will be thrown into "the lake of fire" (v.14); that lake is simply a metaphor for the combustion that happens to all those unstable atoms rushing into the presence of God's pure stable energy to take his new city from Him (see Rev. 20:7-9). This is poetic imagery, not literal, John is trying to describe what he saw, and if you want some exciting reading, read the whole chapter.

So why haven't we questioned this before? We didn't have the perspective. Our collective consciousness thought *God does what He wants because He is God.* We thought the fear of God was literal. Most people served God from fear—but that's not God's way! Now we know that another translation is more accurate: fear is best translated reverence or respect.

So why did God allow this? Because to protect our freedom, God has to leave hooks to hang doubt on. They can't make everything completely plain until someone asks. Some things have to be shrouded in mystery until we start questioning and searching for a better understanding—because They are protecting true freedom.

I don't suppose I am the first one to question or understand this, just one who dares to interpret scripture this way, write it down and publish it. So how do I understand these plagues as being from God and yet caused by Satan? It harks back to episode one.

There is a war going on in the universe over whether God is good and fit to rule. Since They were challenged, God put Themselves on trial. The last part of that war is being battled out on earth. So imagine the council in heaven that laid out the plans and permission for Egypt's demise under Amenhotep II (similar to the one over Job.) I'm

128

guessing it happened 400 years earlier when God made the covenant with Abraham, or before.

**The Council Over Egypt**

Imagine we are hearing Ruach speaking with Abba and Adonai about fulfilling Their covenant promise.

"Here again is another huge risk we have to take. When We hand over Egypt and Amenhotep to Satan, even though we allow the dark side to destroy them, it is going to look like We do it. Even Moses, though he will understand by the end, won't at the time. And when he writes it, that's how it will sound: 'God is bringing plagues, death and destruction to Egypt.' That's how they will interpret it."

"I'm afraid if we try to give Moses another backstory "revelation" like we will do for Job and his story, the dark side will say we've taken advantage against them, making it too plain and unfair for freedom," responds Abba.

Adonai suggests that they invite Satan to the representatives' council when they announce the plan to take Israel out of Egypt. "I'm sure you are right about their accusations, but inviting their participation in Israel's rescue will give us the perfect platform to set the rules for what Satan can and can't do to Egypt." And the others agree.

## 400 Years Later

We join the Godhead again 400 years (of our time) later discussing the details of Their plan on the brink of fulfilling the promise, before calling the council of representatives together.

"As you know, Satan has already been working hard to foil our plans." Adonai opens the conversation. "He was sure Moses was our deliverer, and that we were going to take them out peacefully under Hatshepsut, so he caused the Israelites to feel complacent about leaving, and fearful of the unknown, telling them, "Life isn't that bad here." When Moses tried to talk to them about it, they didn't trust him—thought he was a prince grabbing for power."

Ruach continues, "Yes, and before that, Satan got Moses convinced we were going to use his skill as an army commander, and then triggered him to kill the Egyptian to show his people he was ready to lead them out—adding to their distrust!"

"While I *would have* preferred to lead them out peacefully under his mother Hatshepsut, Moses didn't really know Us well enough then. He would

130

have tried to get them to fight if they were opposed. They would have been overwhelmed with fear and discouragement."

Abba adds, "They would have left Egypt as paupers then. This way, the Egyptians will respect them, ask them to leave, and deck them out to worship their fearsome god! And Moses needed all that time with you and the sheep, Ruach. He is ready to do it our way now."

Ruach chuckles. "Well, he is ready to listen to me and Adonai, and he will be awed, by the time they leave."

"I admit the wow factor isn't the best way to get worship, but it is the best for creating awe," granted Abba, "and all these humans have become so insensitive. And that little Pharaoh is just about hopeless!"

"A little bit of wow won't hurt, unless they get too scared. It will take that to get them out from under Amenhotep's control," assures Ruach.

"Yes," agreed Adonai. "Israel has been wondering why We haven't come to their rescue for some time now. This way they will leave proud to be Adonai's people! Ready? Let's go deal with 'Our Amenhotep'."

### The Representatives Council

Abba presides this time, and begins with, "We are ready to deliver Abraham's descendants from Egypt. And we have decided to let your side have a part in it, Satan," He says it looking at him, then quickly looks at someone else. It is hard to see His still-beloved child looking so dark and raggedy.

"There will be specific boundaries on what you can and can't do. You may cause discomfort, even disease, but you may not take human life until the hail and last plague, and then only from those who don't listen, and the first born from those who won't use our symbol of protection. You may attack their animals, their gods, even cause ruin to their crops, but you have to tell Us your plan ahead of time and get Our approval, and you can only do it on Our signal, agreed?"

"Agreed," says Satan, initially squirming at being so exposed, and then thinking how he can milk this to make God look bad before the whole universe. *I will carry this off with pleasure!*

And then he leaves, and Abba asks the worlds' representatives council if they have any questions before they adjourn. Unfortunately, only a few picked up on Satan being exposed as the destroyer.

## Back to the Flies

And that is how Satan became "Lord of the Flies," at least in my mind.

The third plague started by God telling Moses, "Go to Pharaoh at the river tomorrow morning and say, 'Adonai says 'Let my people go that they may serve Me. And if you don't, tomorrow you will have swarms of flies all through your land. But know that I will make a distinction between My people and yours, and there shall be no flies on their land, so that you know I AM Lord of all the earth.'"

Moses and Aaron went to the river, and spoke God's words to Pharaoh. And the next day flies were everywhere in Egypt, even the ground was black with them. But there were no flies in Israelite homes or in Goshen which was considered "Israeli land."

Would God Do That?

Chapter 12

# Would God Do That?

## Exodus 8:21-9:35

*Elohim allows a lot that They do **not** cause.*

The next morning, Pharaoh wakes up to a fly biting his eyelid, flies sitting all over his bed. He tries to be dismissive about it, but Dog Fly bites are painful, and if they get infected can be serious. (The translators of the Septuagint, aka the LXX, lived in Egypt, and equated this plague to Dog Flies.)

The record says the land was destroyed by them. That is serious, and was the trigger for me thinking about God causing the plagues, which become more severe with each one. Judgments against their gods? Yes, against their terrorist king? Yes, against all the people and the land? If they have had time to know God, yes. But even then, does God destroy? His unveiled Presence, His energy destroys instability (especially evil), yes, but do *They* cause suffering? Do They author destruction?

I don't think so. I think it is incompatible with who They are. And I think *what They do* has to be compatible with *who They are*—Their character as God. They never wanted separation from us, never wanted anything in the universe but love and life, but in order to have freedom, evil had to be at least a remote possibility.

Now that evil **is** a reality, having been activated by their most-gifted creature, Lucifer, they will allow evil's 'king' (now Satan) to work within Their boundaries. This is largely what Job taught us: Satan couldn't touch even a hair on Their man's camel without permission.

So Satan and his dark angels (now demons) are at work, doing what they love, doing their best to bring grievous suffering and make it look like God is the author of it. He has been given the power of suffering and death. But when God takes it away, it will be gone.

Pharaoh, by noon that day, is losing his mind. He has sent a spy to Goshen, and sure enough, there are no flies there. But around him, everywhere people are bitten and crying and wailing. He can't take it, so he sends a messenger for Moses and Aaron, who come back with the messenger.

He takes them straight into the king who says, "Go and sacrifice to your God here in Egypt."

"That wouldn't be right," says Moses through Aaron. "We would be doing abominations according to the Egyptians, by sacrificing what they consider gods. Wouldn't they stone us?"

Pharaoh nods in spite of himself. He knows what Moses says is truth.

So Moses continues, "We will go three days' journey into the wilderness and sacrifice to Adonai as He has commanded us."

"I will let you go, only don't go far away." (He shows he is worried about losing his workforce.) "And ask Adonai to take away the flies."

"I will go out and ask Adonai to remove the flies tomorrow at sunrise; only don't deal deceitfully in giving your word this time." And Moses and Aaron leave the palace.

Moses asks God, "Please take away these flies tomorrow so Pharaoh knows that you are God."

The next morning the flies are all dead at sunrise and the cleanup begins. By 8:00 am. Pharaoh has changed his mind. (I can imagine Satan is having fun with this causing fear of losing his workforce.) And he sends a message to Moses. "You can't go."

## Pestilence with an Out

A few days after the cleanup, Adonai sends Moses to Pharaoh with another warning, "Let my people go to serve Me or tomorrow the hand of the Lord will bring disease on all the livestock in the field and they will die. (His hand allows the Lord of the Flies to act.) But there will be no disease on the livestock of My people."

The word pestilence means plague by itself, usually referring to illness or disease. This time it is called Murrain. It only effects animals, but it kills them. But God has said only those in the field.

Egypt doesn't have to go through this. They can bring them in out of the field. God gives Amenhotep until tomorrow, to relent, but Pharaoh is getting harder with every passing choice of resistance.

And the next day all the livestock of Egypt die, except those who heeded the warning and got their animals out of the field and into their barns. Notice how God provides for even Egyptians who listen to His warning! When Pharaoh inquires, all of Israel's cattle are fine. Now he is defiant.

Adonai knows that Satan's next move is boils, so he sends Moses and Aaron to Pharaoh at the river with handfuls of ashes and instructs Aaron to throw them into the air in front of Pharaoh.

"Tell him it will become boils on both men and animals throughout your land."

They do it, and even the magicians break out with boils and leave in pain. Even Pharaoh has boils, but he is angry and figures *they will heal; I will not give in; I will not let Israel go*.

## The Confrontation Ramps Up

After the boils have run their course, God again sends Moses and Aaron to Pharaoh. This time it is direct confrontation.

Moses and Aaron meet Pharaoh at the river and say, "The God of the Hebrews says, 'Let my people go to serve Me, and if you don't, I will release My plagues to your heart, and on your people and servants, so that you will know there is no god like Me, and My name will be known in all the earth.

'Surely you know by now that I could have wiped Egypt off the ground long ago, without a trace left. However, I let you stand because I wanted to show My kindness and My power through you. You have known of My kindness, that is meant to lead you to change, because of My blessings to your country through Joseph and Hatshepsut, Moses' Egyptian mother. You thought I was weak because you oppressed My people, but now it is time for you to let them go, and yet you exalt yourself against Me, instead of acknowledging Me. So tomorrow morning at this time, I will cause a hailstorm the likes of which has never been seen in Egypt for its severity.

'Send word out to your people in all your land, today, to bring in their animals and servants, and take shelter themselves. For tomorrow whatever has not taken shelter and is in the field will die.'"

Pharaoh smirks while they speak, and then they turn on their heels and walk away, but there is a hint of terror left in his heart. Yet he says to his servants, "Send out word if you want to, but I will not be afraid of their god!"

The next morning, Moses stretches out the rod of God and lightning and thunder and hail begin on the land of Egypt; hail so large and so thick that

140

it's killing everything in the fields, even to splintering all the trees. Only in Goshen is there no hail. And his people in Tanis have stayed home and brought their animals in.

Pharaoh has never seen anything like this. He didn't even take his customary trip to the river that morning. (He's getting it.) He is terrified at the immediate and simultaneous pounding of crashing thunder, lightning and hail. The sky is black but the air is white with hail, and constantly lit up by flashes of lightning. Nobody can ever remember seeing or hearing a storm like this one. There are fire balls running on the ground!

The loss to the country is great. But even Egyptians who have taken shelter for themselves and their animals are spared, just as God said they would be.

**The Kindness of God**

And notice the kindness of God here: two crops, flax and barley are destroyed. The barley is ready to harvest; the flax is in bloom (so it is early February by now), but the wheat and spelt are young enough that they aren't ruined. That kind of hail should have killed all of it, but He spared the ones that weren't ripe.

Notice these metaphors all throughout: protection and provision for those who weren't "ripe" and for those who listened. It reminds me of Psalm 91; did you know that Moses wrote that Psalm and 90? This gives it new meaning. He had witnessed what he was describing. Paul expressed it succinctly much later in his letter to the Romans, when he said, "...Don't you know the kindness of God is meant to lead you to repentance?" (Romans 2:5)

It also struck me just now that the metaphor of the rod becoming the serpent has a purpose. Adonai called it "the rod of God"—it was just Moses' shepherd staff. But when Moses let go of it, it became God's instrument of judgment—and a metaphor for Satan, a death-carrying snake. When Moses or Aaron picked it up, it was just a rod again. When it was stretched out at God's command, it became the signal to Satan that he and his minions could act. And when Moses prayed and asked God to take control, Satan had to stop.

The same symbol was used later in the wilderness when the Israelites complained about God, and the serpents that lived there begin biting them. Before that, they'd been protected from them. Once bitten, they had to look at a gold serpent on a cross to acknowledge they had separated from God, and had been bitten by the death-dealing enemy and needed a remedy.

It's as if God is always and forever saying, "Just acknowledge Me. I won't even force you to follow, but just acknowledge My reality and your need of protection and I will protect you."

Pharaoh's issue was over power and control. And for all of us it is pretty much a lesser form of the same thing: *I want to do it my way!* And do you know what God's wrath is? Scripturally it is defined as God saying, "OK then, have it your way. But I can't protect you from the consequences." That is the severity of God— letting go. The scariest thing about God (Their wrath) is that They will let us leave. They honor our choices.[xix]

It came down to a power struggle between the God of Israel and the king of Egypt. And all who in Egypt believed God was telling the truth was spared from the judgments God sent through Satan.

A whole day of this hail storm and Amenhotep's nerves are jangled. He sends his servants, carrying shields over their heads, to fetch Moses and Aaron. They come to the palace, no need of shields above them, and he says to them, "I have sinned this

143

time. Adonai is right and I and my people are wrong. Ask your God to take away this storm, it has been enough. I will let you go. You shall not stay."

Moses replies with truth, "As soon as I am out of the palace courts, I will lift my hands to Adonai, and the storm and hail will stop so that you may know that the earth is Adonai's.

"But I know you, and I know that you and your servants still don't reverence the Lord." And with that they walk out, confident of protection, while the king's court watches in awe—amazed at their protection.

Moses did just as he said he would, and God honored him and the storm stopped. And Pharaoh did just as Moses said he would, and the next day he changed his mind and sent a message to Moses, "You can't leave."

Chapter 13

# The Power Struggle Ends

## Exodus 10:1-12:29

*The power struggle with God is always lost*

*because if you win, you lose your self, your true*

*self.*

"Moses," says God the next week, "go to Pharaoh and confront him again. My confrontations and convictions have so hardened him, that he will not let you go until I really show my power in a way that hits his heart. He will be ruined, along with his land, but at least my people will be impressed beyond a doubt that I am their deliverer and God of all the earth. You may tell your children and grandchildren about the wonders I did for them in Egypt so that they will all know and remember I

145

AM Adonai—their redeemer. There will be three more plagues, and the last one will finish Pharaoh's resistance. The world will hear of Me."

Moses gets up and goes to get Aaron, and they are off to the palace. Pharaoh even hates to see them coming, and he steels himself for the confrontation, wondering what it will be this time.

Moses and Aaron deliver their message. "This is what Adonai the God of the Hebrews says, 'How long will you resist and refuse to be taught by Me? Let My people go and serve Me, or I will bring locusts into your borders to cover the ground and eat whatever escaped the hail. They will be in your house and your people's houses. No one, not even your old men, will have seen anything like this." And then they turn around and walk out.

Pharaoh's servants and advisors say to him, "How long will you let this man torment us? Send the men to serve their God! Don't you realize that our land is being destroyed?"

Then messengers are sent after Moses and Aaron to bring them back, and Amenhotep says to them, "Go serve your God. But who will be going?"

"We will go with our young and old, our flocks and our herds to make a feast for Adonai."

146

"You will need your God's blessing if I ever let you go with your little ones! You are planning deceit—I can see it on your face. Go now with your men and serve Adonai! That is what you've been asking for." And his attendants grab their arms and usher them out, mindful of the power these two prophets have.

No sooner are they outside and God speaks, "Stretch out your rod and let the locusts come, and they will devour what the hail has left." So Moses does, and the east wind begins to blow. Locusts usually come on a South wind to Egypt, but this is an east wind that brings them from their breeding ground in Arabia, hence the time it takes to blow them in.[xx]

It blows all day and all that night, and the next morning everything is covered with locusts. The noise of them is like a fire crackling or rain pouring, and they eat every green thing that is left.

Pharaoh quickly calls for Moses and Aaron and says, "I have sinned against Adonai and you. Forgive me this once, and please ask your God to take this death away from me!"

Moses leaves and prays, and Adonai turns the east wind into a west wind, and it carries off the locusts into the Red Sea. Not one locust is left.

But of course, Pharaoh's repentance is not the kind that radically changes the heart; it is only good until the consequences are gone. And God, Moses, and Aaron know this. And so it happens again. Pharaoh changes his mind.

A week passes and Adonai says to Moses, "Stretch out your hand and bring darkness that can be felt to cover the land for three days." Moses does, and darkness settles on the land of Egypt.

It is so dark that they can't even see each other, and nothing can be done. They can't even see to move, so most of them stay in bed. It is so dark that it feels oppressive, even difficult to breathe. (This makes most commentators think it was a sandstorm which could last three days, and the fine sand made it hard to breathe. But others think the sand would have been mentioned, just as the hail was, if that had been the case.) All the children of Israel have light in their houses as Pharaoh soon learns. And it isn't the light of lanterns.

**Getting Ready for Passover**

Adonai had already told Moses that there would be one more plague, and he spends the days of darkness when no one can work, meeting with the elders and getting the Israelites prepped for their departure as he has been instructed. Great organization will be needed with so many people.

He tells them, "God is shifting the whole calendar based on your new identity as Adonai's people. The month of Abib (April) is to be the first month of the year from now on, and on the tenth of that month each man is to select a lamb for his family. If you are a small family, two families can share a lamb, but it must be without defect and a year old male. If you don't have a lamb you may use a goat.

"At sunset on the 14th day, the father acting as priest is to cut its throat and drain its blood into a basin and use hyssop (an herb) to put it on the two side posts and the top crossbeam of the doorway. You are then to roast it whole over a fire and eat it with unleavened bread and bitter herbs, but do not boil it or eat it raw. If you have anything left over you are to burn it and not try to keep it till morning or take it with you. (Again protecting them from disease.)

"You are to eat it fully clothed with your traveling clothes on, including your shoes, ready to go, because that night Adonai Himself will come to supervise and make sure the Destroyer only enters houses that are not marked with blood. (12:23)

"This will be an enduring feast called Passover, always kept as a memorial of Adonai's protection on the 14$^{th}$ day of April. For seven days you are to eat unleavened bread. On the first day you must remove all leaven or yeast from your homes. (Yeast was a symbol of sin because fermentation is the first step in decay, and how it changes the nature of the dough so quickly.)

"You will do no work on the first day which is to be a day of corporate worship and rest, and the same is the ending or seventh day. The only work you may do those days is preparing food. This will be a lasting celebration for you."

**The Darkness gets to Pharaoh**

Pharaoh calls for Moses on the third day (he must have had lanterns.) "Go serve your God and take your little ones too, but let your flocks stay here." Now it's obvious he is afraid of losing his workforce. He wants collateral.

But Moses has gotten strong and sure of Adonai, and he answers, "We do not know what Adonai will ask us to sacrifice, and we will need to eat, so we will take all our animals—not a hoof will be left behind."

You don't say that to the king and get away with it, and Pharaoh is angry and hard. "Get out of my sight! And never come to me again, for the day you see my face again you will die!"

But Moses isn't moved. "You have spoken well," he responds, "we are just about done here."

## The Last Plague

After leaving Pharaoh, Adonai sends Moses to the Israelites. "Tell them to ask their neighbors, the women and the men, for articles of silver and gold and fine clothes to dress your families for My festival." (Pictorials show that the men wore just as much jewelry as the women at that time.)

And the Egyptians respond because Adonai gives the Israelites favor. The plagues have caused even the taskmasters to treat those under them with more respect. In fact, all the people in the land revere Moses and they want to give to his cause. He has defeated their gods, and is on at least the same level, if not higher in their minds, than Pharaoh. It's as if they can't give them enough, and give clothes, fabrics and jewelry in abundance.

That same day Moses goes to the elders and asks them to tell every household to select their lamb and keep him in readiness for the 14th.

Some of the Egyptians are so impressed with the Hebrew God that they come and ask if they can stay in their houses and be protected and leave Egypt with them. Certainly they are welcomed, because that is who God is—always welcoming to anyone who wants to be included. And that is how it happens that many Egyptians leave with the Israelites. Some from awe and some from fear of what God will yet do to Egypt.

Satan loves fear in any form and doesn't try to turn it into fear of the Israelites or their God because he has plans for this "mixed multitude." They will be very useful to him when the going gets tough. It hasn't escaped his notice that God is not threatened by suffering, and he knows Adonai will allow some difficult times to grow the peoples' confidence and faith in Him. The enemy plans to introduce discontent and discouragement from Egyptian spouses, and the newbies who are there for selfish reasons, or from fear, or the desire to escape. Expressions of doubt and discouragement have historically been among his best tools.

On the morning of the 14th all of Israel is called together and Moses repeats Adonai's instructions to them for this day and this night. "It is important that you do everything just as He has told you so

He can protect you. Do not leave your houses once you have put the blood on the doorway and have roasted the lamb.

"This is serious. We are not celebrating yet, so eat in readiness to leave. Everything you are taking should be packed and ready by this time. At midnight the Destroyer [xxi] will kill all of the firstborn in Egypt who are not protected by Adonai's symbol of redemption. He knew it would take this to get Pharaoh to agree to your release, but He wanted to give him and the Egyptians a chance to know him and inquire, so He has taken us through these last six months of showing his wonders.

(The whole thing must have started in October with approximately a week in between plagues because the hail storm was early February--the flax was in bloom.)

"It was partly for you to know His greatness and goodness as well, and to fill you with awe at His power and His kindness toward you, and to all who respond to Him. But tonight it will be over. And Pharaoh and the people will ask us to leave. There will be terrible disaster and distress as God withdraws his protection from Egypt, steps back and allows the Destroyer to do his horrible work."

The people are solemn as they go to their homes. Everything is changing. Yes they feel glad, to be so loved, but they are also sad for the terrible loss that will come to every home in Egypt—excepting those who have come to the Hebrews asking for protection.

At midnight, a great cry goes up from the palace and extends through every unprotected home in the land, as they discover their firstborn son is suddenly overcome with a strange illness and quickly dies.

Egypt is filled with shrieks, wailing and mourning.

Chapter 14

# "Get Out!"

## Exodus 12:30-14:4

*Conversions from fear don't last long.*

A devastated Amenhotep hastily sends for Moses and Aaron, and when they arrive, he says, "Leave! Take everything and everyone as you have said and get out! Leave us, and bless me too." (He finally acknowledges Adonai's supremacy.)

They leave Pharaoh's palace, and give the signal from the ram's horn.

The large Hebrew community has been instructed when and how to prepare and is ready to go. Their neighbors have come, urging them to leave, giving them more gifts, "Go, before we are all dead," they beg.

The Israelites hear the horn, and in the dark, torches began to move toward the meeting place in groups of 50. Every family walks out to join the others.

As they leave the city they follow Moses, who is carrying the bones of Joseph, procured and put in a box according to his brothers' promise, handed down as a prophecy of deliverance. (Archaeology has unearthed a pyramid tomb at Tanis with a huge Asiatic statue and no bones.)[xxii]

One by one this procession realizes that it is much lighter than the light of their torches, *is it morning already?* they wonder, and then notice that a huge fiery cloud is following them, lighting up the night to be like day. In awe they put out their torches, now unneeded, as word spreads from Moses back, "This is the presence of Adonai."

God follows them all the way from Tanis down to Succoth in Goshen, a distance of 32 miles, as they walk from about 1:00 a.m. until after sunrise when their rearguard cloud of fire becomes a pillar of cloud in front. They are giddy with excitement. *It's finally happening! We are leaving Egypt! We are free! Adonai lights our way and leads us!*

The people in Succoth had been instructed not to leave their homes until Moses and Aaron with the people from Tanis arrive, and they fall asleep.

Moses says later that Succoth in Goshen was their first camp, showing God's care. No one is worried about Pharaoh stopping them now! The people from Tanis excitedly tell their friends and relatives at Succoth, how they left in the middle of the night and that the cloud they see was a fire that followed them all the way making the night as bright as day! God had to empower them with great infusions of endorphins, or how could they have walked 30 miles on no sleep?

But then it may have seemed like a couple of hours to them, since they were so filled with awe. (I remember this same experience in writing the first episode of this series. I thought it was about two and a half hours of writing, and when I looked at the clock it had been seven hours!)

Surely all are eager to get on their way the next morning. The women are up early and begin making unleavened bread dough for breakfast, but before they can get it baked, the rams horn sounds; so they tie the dough up in shawls in their kneading troughs (some sort of long dish for

157

kneading bread), put it on their shoulders and leave, in their previously arranged groups of 50.

Moses account says they left Egypt "harnessed" (it's usually translated "armed" which makes no sense, but probably means well-organized—with that many people you would have to be—and they were led by a military general!)

Several miles from Succoth, Israel camps at Etham on the edge of the desert. Every family has a tent and knows exactly where to put it. The tribe of Judah leaves first after the horn blows, and camps first to the east whenever they camp, beside them camp Issachar and Zebulun. Reuben comes next and camps to the South with two other tribes, and so on, until finally Dan is last (Numbers 2).

So far, no fears are roused back at the palace, this is what Pharaoh expected. Besides, he is still reeling from grief. The whole country is.

Adonai knows the people need rest and also encouragement. Notwithstanding the endorphins He certainly gave them, exhaustion tends to dis-spirit people. He tells Moses to lead a worship service in the morning in which he reiterates the meaning of the symbols of the Passover. Adonai wants them to revisit the greatness and power of their God. Awe does more to impress people than any other emotion. And praise raises spirits.

**Worship**

Moses calls his leaders to have the people come and sit in a semi-circle; they are going to worship God. Adonai has told Moses, "Consecrate to Me all the firstborn of Israel, both men and animals, today."

The people come from their tents and Moses says, "Remember this day—the day Adonai took you out of Egyptian slavery by His own strong hand, out of bondage. You are to remember and celebrate the symbols of His Passover when He didn't allow the Destroyer to enter your homes, but caused him to pass over your houses because of your faith in applying the blood. And for the next seven days you will eat no yeast.

I have wondered, h*ow did Moses talk to so many people?* Maybe some sort of ram's horn makes a good megaphone. Or maybe God had them stop where there was always a natural amphitheater—hillsides are great for magnifying sound. Or it could be that every so-many-yards the prince or leader of the tribe stood and passed on Moses' words. Moses has been an army general. It wasn't

159

uncommon for armies to have 10,000 men. He knows how to do this, and continues,

"This is April, and you are leaving Egypt. When Adonai brings you into your own land flowing with plenty, a land which He is taking from other nations to give to you, as He promised Abraham, you are to observe this celebration during this month. For seven days from the 14$^{th}$ day, you shall eat no leavened bread. And the seventh day, is to be a feast to Adonai. No yeast is to be found within your homes during this week. When you roast the Passover lamb, you are not to break any of its bones, and no foreigner may eat of it.

"And when your children ask you why these days and foods are special, you will tell them, 'It is because of what Adonai did for me when I came out of Egypt.'

So it will be like a brand on your hand or, better, in your frontal lobe, so that the law of Adonai may fill you with wonder, making you want to talk about it. For with a strong hand He brought you out of Egypt. You are to keep this fresh with a ritual of remembrance every year when you come into the land of the Canaanites which He swore to give you.

"So today we consecrate every first born man and animal to Adonai, and every year you will do the same. If your son asks 'Why are you doing this?' You say, 'With his strength Adonai brought us out of slavery in Egypt. When Pharaoh refused to let us go, Adonai allowed the Destroyer to kill all of the firstborn of men and animals, but he protected you and caused the Destroyer to pass over us. So I sacrifice all of the firstborn male animals, but I redeem my firstborn son.'

"And when you celebrate the Passover in your own land, only those who are willing to join your community through the rite of circumcision will be allowed to eat the Passover."

After Moses finished speaking, all the first-born males, man or animal, were set aside for the use of the Lord, making them holy. (They were later replaced by the Levites.)

**Back on the Way**

The Hebrews are told again that the cloud giving them light, so they can see at night, is Adonai; sometimes leading them and other times above them as a shield from the sun. When it moves they move. When it stops, they camp. It stopped on the edge of the wilderness at Etham, and after camping and worshipping, God says to Moses,

"Tell My children, we are going back north to camp before Pihahiroth, between Migdol and the sea, opposite Baal-zephon. Pharaoh will hear and say that you are lost in the land, 'The wilderness has confused and swallowed them,' and I will harden his heart, and he will follow after them. But I will get honor from it and the Egyptians will know that I am God."

## Who Hardened Pharaoh?

Another note on hardening Pharaoh's heart since it is repeated here: Again, God allows everyone freedom to follow His leading or reject it. God's love affects us—either it softens or hardens hearts. The same sun hardens clay and melts butter. Our hearts harden by resistance. But God always takes responsibility for what happens. He doesn't even expose Satan here! They are so generous.

Adonai's directions are specific, obviously given to one who is familiar with Egypt. (Migdol was one of several military outposts—they are passing right under military noses!) He takes them north, but He doesn't just lead them expecting them to follow because He is God, he tells them ahead where they are going.

Of course, God knows exactly what He is doing, but many people from "the mixed multitude" aren't so sure. Now these especially began to wonder, *why are we going north? And is this cloud really their God or just a cloud? Or worse, some bad omen? Why aren't we going East on the trade route--the shortest distance through Philistine country, which normally takes 11 days?* They have come with the Israelis from fear, or desire to leave Egypt. (Maybe some of them were slaves as spoils of war before the Hebrews came.)

Adonai knows that if Israel immediately sees even the threat of war, they will faint, and that the Philistines will see them as escaping slaves, free for the taking because they are in their land. And if the Israelites don't start back to their homes in Egypt, they will want to.

God could have rescued them powerfully from the Philistines also, but there are things to consider. One huge one is the need for time for the Hebrews to know God and see Him act for them so they can learn to trust Him. For Gods' perspective we must jump back to another council that the Three of Them had earlier.

## God's Compassionate Plan

"I know we could show wonders to the Philistines about who we are," said Adonai, "but they haven't recently had the same opportunities as the

Egyptians, who will soon after Israel's exodus decide to pursue them. And furthermore our current agreement with the dark side is over Egypt."

"Right," Ruach had agreed. "According to the Rules of Engagement, if Satan stirs up the Philistines, which will be very easy to do as they love to fight, they are inside their limits. The Philistines will make war on Israel and carry off their women, children and animals as spoil, unless we stop them. And as long as the dark side is working through humans, they are within the guidelines, and we are at a disadvantage. We didn't make an agreement to hand over the Philistines to them. Abimelech and his sons were good men, and listened to Us, even helping Us by confronting Abraham and Isaac. I'm not ready to give them over to Satan to destroy."

"I agree." added Adonai. "And if the Philistines come after Our people, Israel will want to return to Egypt, and think We are no gods at all. They don't know Us any better than the Philistines. We need to do something different. Let's take them up to the North, there's space for them to camp by the sea between the outpost and the mountain, and when Pharaoh comes after them, we will pile up

164

the water for Moses and take them through the sea. They will remember that for a while!"

"I concur," finished Abba. I'm sure Satan will lead Pharaoh's troops into the river bed after the Israelites, and We will let go of the water. That will finish off Amenhotep, his advisors, great leaders, and priests right in front of their god Baal at Baal-zephon. All of this will give his second son pause to think about Us and starting in another direction, when he comes to the throne."

But of these facts the Israelites, and the "mixed" crowd with them, are ignorant. They begin to see sinister meaning in the cloud after a few days.

### *What is Going On?*

Satan has all of his dark angels ready, whispering doubts: *Maybe that cloud really isn't their god. Maybe this is a big hoax. We've heard of Moses, what if he's come back for revenge with a maniacal power trip!*

*Why look, now we are locked in by the sea on one side, the mountain on the other, and a shrine to the Egyptian god Baal! We're caught between gods!*

Moses, by this time knows he can trust God, and he is calm and not afraid, even when God takes them into a corner, with the Red Sea on two sides,

165

the mountain on the other and the Egyptians behind them. The six months of plagues to Egypt were meant to strengthen the Hebrews' faith, but it hasn't, as yet, been tested in the way that brings a chance for growth and choice. This is the only kind of testing God does, more accurately called assaying.

.

Chapter 15

# "Stand Still and See!"

## Exodus 14:5-15:21

*"When God wants to do something amazing, He starts with the impossible.*

The Egyptians, men especially, are trying to control their grief by explaining what has happened. It is human to intellectualize. In a few days, Pharaoh's advisors began working on him, saying, "Why did we let our whole workforce go?" And "Why did we attribute the loss of our sons to their god?"

"Yes," says another. "Everything we've been through in the past six months could all be explained by natural causes starting a chain reaction from the red algae in the Nile they called blood. Their god? Ha! They got us scared; that's all. And now we have let our best builders go!"

"And we've heard from the outposts that they are going north and east toward Baal-zephon," adds another. They aren't coming back! The three days you gave them are past."

"They must be lost!" says Pharaoh. "They are wandering around in confusion, and can't find their way through the wilderness. They would be going east if they were escaping. What will we look like to other nations if we allow our slaves to walk away or die? We must make a great recovery of them and save our reputation!" And with that he orders his 600 chariots to get ready, along with all the other chariots.

He himself will lead the recovery, accompanied by all his advisors and great leaders, eager to go. They will take the priests with them too, to make sure their mission is successful.

Approximately 2,000,000 Hebrews have just arrived at their destination and set up camp. They've had one good night's sleep, when the campers on the outer edge see the sun glinting off of armor, and realize an army is approaching! The chariots of Egypt are coming from Tanis and panic sweeps through the camp! This is surely Pharaoh coming to kill them or force them back into slavery, and they are terrified. There is no way out! The sea is on the north and east, the mountain on the south and the Egyptians coming from the west.

A few cry to God, but others start coming to Moses saying, "Did you bring us out here to die because there weren't enough graves in Egypt? Didn't we say you should leave us alone to serve the Egyptians? That would have been better than dying out here!"

Especially those who are not Israelis get the people stirred up, and Moses goes to Adonai, saying, "Do something! These people don't know You, and they are driving me crazy!"

God answers Moses, "Why are you crying to Me? *You* know Me! Tell the people to go forward, and stretch out your rod over the waters and it will part for you, and you will walk through the sea on dry ground."

"Look up!" Moses directs the people's attention to the cloud that is lifting from the front by the sea and moving back over them, becoming a pillar between them and the Egyptians just as the sun is setting. They can no longer see the armies or the setting sun glinting off of chariots and armor. And then as darkness falls swiftly their side of the cloud becomes bright as it has before when they have needed light at night.

Moses blows the ram's horn calling them into their worship half-circle. (Maybe it forms up the rock mountain?) He points at the back of their pillar of light. It is black. "Do you see that your assailants have total darkness while we are blessed with light? Have no fear. Adonai has not brought you into the desert to kill you, but to show you his power and glory. He will fight for you and you will not have to lift a finger. The Egyptians you have seen today, you will never see alive again, and all you have to do is be still."

Their hope revives as they see their light with the darkness all around them, and calm comes over them. Moses informs them that God has told him to stretch his rod over the sea and it will part for them to cross. For months they have been hearing about Moses' rod in Egypt.

"Adonai has told me we are to cross through the sea on dry ground," and with that he walks several yards and lifts his rod over the sea, and the water parts, a miraculous wind blowing straight through to the east, piling up the water and drying the ground.

He walks back and directs them to sleep while the wind dries their path, saying, "When you hear the ram's horn, get ready, at the second one get into walking formation with your families, flocks and possessions, and we will walk through this sea."

The people gaping in awe, move to their places to sleep until they hear the rams horn, they pack up, ready to go, and let the sound of the wind lull them to sleep.

Several hours later, (I like to think they slept six hours and were awakened about midnight like the Passover, it was before the morning watch which starts at 3:00 a.m.) with God's light making it like day the ram's horn is heard, waking everyone, and the people get ready to move. The leader of each group of 50 checks to make sure everyone of their group is there.

## Walk Out Your Faith

With the sound of the second horn, the cloud moves to the sea again, and the walls of water light up. The people move forward, led by Moses and walk down onto the dry bottom of the Sea of Reeds (usually called the Red Sea.) What a hike that was on a wide swath between two live aquariums! An experience they would never

171

forget—their mysterious God-light shining off of the water lighting up its plants and fish.

The watchmen for the Egyptians notice that the unusual darkness has lifted and wake Pharaoh and his commanders. They break camp and pursue as soon as it is light. When they reach the Israelite camp, no one is there. At the water, the last of the Israelites are reaching the other side.

The Egyptians arrogantly proceed, not realizing—or choosing to ignore—that this is not a normal occurrence. As soon as they enter between the walls of water, the cloud that has been providing light for the Israelis, moves above them and releases a torrent of rain, complete with lightning and thunder so bad that the earth shook. The chariot wheels get clogged with mud, they clean them and they clog again. Finally, at least one of the brighter commanders says, "Their God, Adonai is fighting for them, let's turn back!" But it is too late, they are too far in. They are stuck in the mud and the storm, and can't get turned around, even though their chariots are made for maneuvering.

It is dawn now, and the Egyptians are all in the depths, when Adonai says to Moses, "Stretch out your rod again and take them out of their misery."

Moses obeys and the walls of water come crashing down covering every chariot, charioteer, and archer. They all died in front of the shrine to one of their main gods—Baal.

Many of Israel's men line the opposite shore, in awe of their deliverance by a God so amazing as their Adonai. The only thing they see of the Egyptians is the bodies of warriors washed up on the shore by the current.

According to Josephus' account,[xxiii] Moses has the men pick the weapons and armor off of the dead bodies, and now Israel really is armed.

**The Response of Praise**

Can you even imagine what they had been through in the last 24 hours! It starts with them wondering why they aren't going the "right" way, but they keep going, being told God is leading them. After they get to their destination, and notice they are locked in on three sides, they see an army of chariots coming after them. Now they are terrified, but Moses calm trust in God helps, and when they see what he points out about the cloud, and see the water roll back and make a path through the sea, hope revives. They actually sleep. They are physically and emotionally exhausted!

They get up and start their walk through the sea (the timing has to be precise) because as soon as the cloud moves and Pharaoh's camp can see anything, they will be coming after them, and chariots can travel faster. Imagine the size and brightness of that cloud! They are in wonder and awe, and a little anxious, as they wait their turn to begin walking between the walls of water. Can you imagine the feelings of the last ones into the sea!

The last families aren't even close to scrambling up the opposite shore, when the Egyptians reach the opposite bank and follow in the path through the water. (Imagine how that felt!) Then comes the storm, as the last of the Israelis come up the east bank, fierce and loud, but there is no rain on them!

After the Egyptian army gets stuck, Adonai tells Moses to stretch out his rod and the waters come crashing down, drowning their pursuers.

Try to imagine that relief! And the freedom they feel. How special they feel having God deliver them supernaturally!

They have been led into their camping formation, and by now they all have their spots. The brave ones come back out to the edge of the sea to see what has happened.

174

The whoops and hollers of victory bring the rest of them to see. Their enemies are all dead, and they feel like singing and dancing once it is realized. By now they have gotten the spoils of armor and stacked it. And they hear the ram's horn calling them into their semi-circle for a worship celebration.

Miriam has sent word through the company— "Every woman who has a timbrel (tambourine), go and get it." Moses leads a triumphant anthem of praise called the song of Moses. His poetic ability, infused by joy and Ruach's melody, brings up the first recorded worship song.

"I will sing to Adonai for He is exalted!

The horse and rider He has thrown into the sea.

The Lord is my strength and my song,

And He has become my salvation.


"This is my God, and I will glorify Him!

My father's God and I will exalt Him!

Adonai is a warrior—Adonai is His name!

Pharaoh's chariots and army He has hurled into the sea.

It continues for thirteen more stanzas about God's might and glorious power, and how the enemy said what he would do, but God blew with His wind and brought their plans to nothing. Now all the nations around will be in awe when they hear how God has worked for His people, when they hear about His strong arm bringing them deliverance, and taking them to their inheritance.

Miriam then leads all the women to the outside of their half-circle playing their tambourines and dancing. As the men sing the song again with Moses, the women repeat each line. Imagine that joyful and triumphant sound!

**God Celebrates Too**

I think Abba comes for a little celebration with Ruach and Adonai after that. First, Their presence brings the storm and They have to shed a few tears over losing a few thousand men they loved (the Egyptians), but then the suffering turns quickly to Joy! They probably do a little dancing and singing Themselves! This was a great triumph over the dark side.

Costly, yes; and yes, it took time. But the huge victory was that They finally, again, have someone who will listen closely enough and believe Them enough to let Them work through him!

True, They would rather have redeemed Israel peacefully under Hatshepsut, but Israel had been

176

too comfortable then to embark on the unknown. And Moses thought deliverance was all about doing it his way as a military general. He didn't know God well enough then to lead so many people who lack self-discipline or faith. Why, they hardly knew God!

Moses himself had had a lot of unlearning to do. Yes, it had taken 40 years, but he had done it! And he will need dependency on God to lead a half-million 6$^{th}$ grade boy scouts (roughly Israel's emotional maturity). Now comes the hard work for Moses.

**Listening In**

"Is he ready for this, Ruach?" Abba asks again. He knows how hard this mass of people will be to manage with Satan's side working on them.

"He will certainly learn to depend on Us now!" Ruach's deep chuckle has a note of melancholy in it. "They will put him to the test again and again. Their memories are so short, and they are so easily distracted and emotionally swayed."

"He will have his hands full!" adds Adonai. "But I feel good about our connection. I think he will be ok. The people—not so much. But this will certainly show the other worlds that freedom is not doing whatever you want as Satan has claimed."

Abba mused, "The best education for them, and the watching universe, will be that their broken natures are the worst kind of bondage. Do you

177

think that they will even be able to understand Our law—even if We simplify it and break it down into rules? I can already guess what Satan is going to do with that!"

"For sure!" agrees Adonai. "But taking them to the cathedral of Sinai will give us some time."

"Count on interference," nods Ruach. "They are already making suggestions and plans to make our grandest sharing event look and feel like another kind of slavery!"

Abba shakes his head. "I'll be so glad when this is all over!"

"I know, and so will I!" Adonai smiles reassuringly at Abba. "It's hard to watch now, I agree, but I will succeed, and Moses will too. They will stretch him, but soon all responders will be singing the Song of Moses and the Lamb![xxiv] And we will get to sing it with them because We have suffered with them.

"You can lead it, Abba! Look ahead to the joy of that **and** having your very own human son! That will give You joy! This suffering will quickly give way to Joy! And we will never have to go through this again! It's worth it. You said so Yourself!"

"So be it," Abba concludes. Give Moses everything he needs. He will be a great symbol of You. Let's do something special for him when You give Our Law. And, why don't We have Jethro bring his wife and boys back, and he can visit for a while after the Amalekites attack. That will encourage him. He admires and loves Jethro and Jethro will give him some wisdom to make his job easier."

"Great idea." Agree the others.

Chapter 16

# Already?

## Exodus 15:22—16:31

*It's hard to believe how quickly
we can forget our experiences of awe!*

After the Red Sea victory, it was all the people could talk about! It was all anyone around within miles and miles could talk about!

"Wow! We've never heard of a god doing anything like that!" everyone said. All the nations around were in awe, (except for the Amalekites).

Why isn't there any Egyptian record of it? Because Egypt never kept records of defeats. None. The only way we know it happened to them is the record left on a stone monument by the son of Amenhotep II who came to the throne unexpectedly. Thutmose IV said the Sphinx told him he would come to the throne after his older

181

brother died mysteriously[xxv] (when the Destroyer didn't pass over). And we get a similar hint in several reliefs found in the Ramesseum at Thebes from about that time, picturing "Hittites" drowning in battle.[xxvi]

If you've ever wondered how long an amazing, incredible experience, one that you will never forget, affects your behavior, here is a study on it.

I'm hoping they stayed and basked in the glory of God's love for the rest of that amazing day and night. In fact, they couldn't have camped there for a few more days to rest because of decomposing bodies, hence putrefied water. So they quickly filled their goatskins and watered their flocks, and the next morning they were on the move again. A source of fresh water with that many people is imperative.

I imagine they were still talking about their amazing deliverance the first and second day, repeating it again and again as they walked. But the third day they ran out of water—even the donkeys that can go three days without, needed water.

Moses, knowing this route, watches with anxiety as the cloud they are following leads right to Marah where the water is bitter. *What is Adonai thinking?* he wonders.

The shouts go up "Water! Water!" and adults and children run to the springs, but it is so bitter they can't drink it! Immediately, those who taste it cry out! "Marah!" (It's bitter!) And others start wailing that they are all going to die!

Seriously? You've had huge miracles to keep you alive, obviously done by God, and you are afraid of dying three days later?

So Moses goes to Adonai, "What do I do now? It's true there is no water that's fit to drink for all the people and animals. What do You want me to do?"

His inquiry must have seemed like music to God, somebody was coming to Him first, before going into panic mode!

"Do you see that little tree over there? Throw it in the water and it will be fit to drink." Moses can hear the smile in His voice. God has a sense of humor.

*Pull up a small tree and throw it in the water? Really?* Moses must have thought?

But he is happy to obey this God who loves unorthodox surprises. So he grabs hold of the small tree and pulls it up and throws it in the water, and then cups his hands and drinks. *Of course!* He isn't surprised, the water is perfectly sweet. The best he has ever tasted.

Then all the people drink and water their flocks, and all is good again. (I wonder how many of them thought to thank Adonai or Moses.)

Adonai thinks *I will have Moses make this a teachable moment,* so He says, "Moses, tell the people, 'Adonai is trying to teach you to trust Him, to see if you will believe He can take care of you. If you will diligently listen to the voice of Adonai, your God, and conform to His ways and commands, He says, 'I will allow none of the diseases to come upon you that I allowed to come on the Egyptians, because I am Adonai who heals you.'"

After camping, Moses calls them together for worship. It's easy now, after another miracle. And he tells them what God told him to say to them. The people are grateful, and again marveling.

The next day is a short travel day. They come to the oasis at Elim where there are twelve springs and seventy date palms. Moses instructs them to go into camp formation. They are going to stay there by the water under the palms for a week and rest. The people are happy. But it only lasts while circumstances are good.

**The Wilderness of Nothing**

May 15 they come to the Wilderness of Sin. (I wondered if it was named after them, but discovered it was already named that because of the barrenness.) There is nothing there. How appropriate, that the Hebrew word for sin means "nothing," or "without." God is fullness; sin is nothing; or worse, a mirage! Sin is the absence of everything, including life—the choice to be without God.

They are on their way to Sinai, as Adonai had told Moses when he talked to him at the burning bush. But it has now been a month since they left Egypt, and the people are getting nervous. Moses account says all the people murmured against him and Aaron.

"If only Adonai had killed us in Egypt when we sat by pots of meat and ate meat and bread until we were full. But you have brought us into the wilderness to kill our entire community and our children by starvation."

If you do the math, it took about 200,000 sheep to feed all those people every evening when they camped.

Yes, they had huge flocks and herds when they left, but a month later they are largely gone—6,000,000 sheep or goats (and a few less than that if cows were used.) Their bags of wheat and spelt and barley which they grind for bread are gone. *So maybe God can make bad water sweet, but can he provide food in the wilderness for 2,000,000 people?* they wonder. Many are skeptical; some are sure He can't.

Moses turns to Adonai, who tells him, "I will rain bread from heaven for you. The people will gather a days' portion every day, so I can see whether they will walk according to My way or not. On the sixth day they will gather twice as much as they gather every other day."

Moses has Aaron call the elders and tell them to tell their tribes, "In the morning Adonai will give you bread to fill you, and in the evening you will have meat to eat. Tomorrow you will know that Adonai has brought you out from the land of Egypt. In the morning you will see His glory. He has heard your murmuring and doubting. Why complain against us? What are we but men like you? Your complaints aren't against us but against God!"

The people are amazed and incredulous; some of them can't believe it. Even Moses prays *how in the world will You find meat for this many people?* He feels Adonai smile and he thinks, *Israel's God loves to do the impossible for His people and create surprises! I can't wait to see this!*

### So You Will Know I AM Leads You

The next morning Moses calls the whole assembly into their worship formation and tells them, "Come near before Adonai because he has heard your complaining."

As he is speaking, they see "their cloud" in the wilderness behind him, and it becomes brighter than day—brighter than anything they have ever seen! Moses sees their faces and turns, they are seeing God's glory, and Adonai speaks to Moses, "I have heard the complaints of the sons of Israel;

tell them at dusk today you will eat meat, and in the morning you will be filled with bread. Then you will know that I am Adonai your God."

Just as the sun begins to set quail walk and fly into the camp, so many that they cover the ground, and everyone roasts quail and eats it that evening, as they marvel at the power and light of Adonai.

I marvel at the goodness of Adonai just thinking about it! How kind, even sweet, He is to meet these people where they are. He knows they need signs and wonders—they need to see God's power and glory with their senses, and He obliges them.

They haven't gone hungry yet, they are only worrying if they will. They are imagining their children dying! I want to say, "Come on! Adonai just saved you from slavery and death!" But they are looking into the future with fear, instead of remembering with gratitude. They could be giving thanks for their experiences of His marvelous care and protection. Adonai has told them He will be with them and take care of them. But if they don't see it with their eyes, they don't believe it.

They forget how he protected their children from the Destroyer in Egypt, how he took them through the Red Sea when there was no way out.

They forget? Not really. It was too huge! They give in to old patterns. Their habitual thoughts are fear and worry. He wants to lift them to a new level of functioning by learning to trust Him, so He must allow difficulties as opportunities to choose to turn to Him in fear or helplessness. The apparent impossibilities are necessary for learning to choose.

Look what I found in an old commentary on this story, written a hundred years ago by a woman,

> "Do we well to be thus unbelieving? Why should we be ungrateful and distrustful? Jesus is our friend; all heaven is interested in our welfare; and our anxiety and fear grieve the Holy Spirit of God...It is not the will of God that his people should be weighed down with care."[xxvii]

Beautiful! All of heaven cares about us!

The next morning there is dew that looks like frost on the ground. When it dries there are small round somethings left. They don't know what it is, and they say to each other, "What is it?" (In Hebrew "Man nu?" so Manna became its name.)

Moses sends word throughout the camp. "This is the bread that Adonai has sent, and this is His instruction: 'Every man is to gather according to his needs, two quarts per person. Every man is to take it for those in his tent. Fix it as you like, but don't leave any over until morning.'"

So the men gather, some less and some more, but when they measure it, they discover that those who gathered less have just enough, and those who gathered more have nothing left over. And every man gathered as much as he thought he needed! It's the fifth miracle of provision, this one symbolizing that your time with God, whether 10 minutes or 2 hours, will be just enough for you.

Some keep Manna overnight. And the next morning it smells putrid and has worms. Moses is angry with them for not following directions; it's like parenting over-controlled children! Freedom makes them challenge everything.

After that, the men gather it for their families every morning and when the sun grows hot it melts! The women can bake it into bread or boil it for porridge, or even pound it into cereal with goat's milk. And it is good tasting—like wafers or cakes made with honey.

On Thursday, Moses says, "Tomorrow you must gather twice as much because none will come on the seventh day, but on Friday night it will keep sweet. So prepare the Manna however you choose and make enough for your needs on the next day because it is a holy Shabbat (Sabbath or rest) to Adonai. (The days didn't have names yet just numbers—Sabbath was an old concept going back to creation and Abraham, but new to most of them. It was lost during the years of slavery.)

The people prepare and keep Manna Friday night and it doesn't spoil. Another reminder every week of Adonai's care and provision. The people are excited. Probably some wondered if it really did

189

spoil overnight before, and tried again, but buried it and didn't tell anyone when it bred worms.

"This will occur every six days." Moses tells them. "On Friday you will always gather twice as much because none will be on the ground on Sabbath."

But some men go out on the seventh day to gather it and there isn't any. And Adonai says to Moses, "I wonder how long they will refuse to acknowledge My leadership and directions. Tell them again to stay inside the camp with their families and rest on My special day, and not to go out to gather food."

Three special gifts were given that week: quail, Manna and the Sabbath. Every single day they had special evidence of God's care in angels providing food (Psalm 78:25). It was so special that later Aaron is instructed to put a measure of Manna in a jar and put it in the ark in front of the Ten Commandments as a reminder of His providence. A symbol of the bread of heaven—Messiah.

Also, He resurrected the Sabbath, as an invitation to remember Him and relate to Him as their leader and provider. They were reminded of the specialness of that day every sixth day when they gathered twice as much Manna and it kept as fresh as it was the day before. The bread of heaven fell every day but Sabbath. It looked like white

190

coriander seed and fed them every day until they went into Canaan.

Isn't it interesting that God gave them work to do in the wilderness to provide for their families. The men gathered Manna and the women prepared it. The children, overseen by the fathers, tended flocks. Work is a good thing, knowing you are needed. It raises self-worth. God knew they needed that! They didn't promote doing nothing.

Adonai was giving them a new identity. That's the reason Sabbath was reinstituted as a weekly celebration of Whose they were, to Whom they belonged; and His power and care. Belonging is another basic need. He wanted to raise their awareness of being God's special people going to their promised land. He was making a nation of slaves to be the prominent nation in the world under His leadership.

Chapter 17

# Not Again!

## Exodus 17

*Would we be like them? Really?*

The camping is now much further South, in the wilderness with two more campsites before they reach Rephidim, so they must be coming up on 40 days—the time God has given to teach them to trust before entering into a covenant with Adonai.

True, that isn't long to learn to trust, but we are talking God, here, with continual evidence of His Presence, giving proof of His love in Manna, and power to provide in meat. None of them thought He could provide quail for so many people. But did they get it? Would they take in the message?

Maybe not. Or was it a fearful few who caused the chaos? Because they came to Rephidim where the cloud stopped, indicating they were to camp, and

193

once again there was no water to drink. So did they go to God? Or at least to Moses and say, "Ask God what we should do about water?"

No. They get demanding. They go to Moses and say, "Give us water to drink!" Oh yeah, an attitude of entitlement is starting. They are definitely teen maturity! Demanding their rights!

"Why are you picking a fight with me?" asks Moses. "And why do you challenge Adonai? Hasn't He shown his care?"

Their attitude is all wrong, and Moses confronts them directly. They've had every need supplied, and yet, where is the gratitude? These particular people don't like his questions and accuse him.

"Why did you bring us out of Egypt? Did you plan to kill us and our children and our cattle with thirst?"

"No, he's going to kill us and take our stuff!" says another.

"Is Adonai among us or not?" shouted some others

Maybe lack of water makes people crazy; they can't blame it on sunstroke, they have their own built-in air-conditioning—Adonai whose cloud keeps them from the desert sun, adds the right amount of moisture. He gives them a nightlight for reassurance of His presence and protection, and more light when needed. But some are voicing

194

fears about the cloud, and scaring others. Fear and negativity can make you crazy.

Moses can see they are beyond reasoning with, so he doesn't even reply. He turns and walks into his tent which he has just finished pitching. He goes directly to Adonai. (See how well *he* has learned!) "What should I do with these people? They are picking up stones and getting so crazy they are ready to stone me!" (Evidently, that was the way Egyptians resolved unwanted situations with outcasts—Moses had told Pharaoh the people would stone them if they offered their sacred cows, remember?)

And Adonai answers, "In front of all the people, take the elders and walk up Horeb carrying your staff. You remember that big rock part way up Horeb; I will stand there in the cloud, and you strike the rock, and water will come out of it so the people can drink."

So Moses calls the elders and taking his staff he walks with them to the big rock a short way up the mountain. In sight of all the people, who see the cloud above the rock become extremely bright, and with the elders beside him, he strikes the rock and a burst of water shoots out and creates a waterfall and a river. All the people are in awe for a moment, and then rush to drink. They bring their animals and take water to their campsites.

(I see another symbol of Messiah. If you've read the New Testament you can't help but think of Jesus calling himself the bread from heaven and the water of life.)

Again I wonder, *Did they say thank you?* Or *I'm sorry?* I doubt the complainers did. It takes mental health to see and admit you are wrong.

But these people weren't raised to focus on gratitude, and those who had come just to get out of Egypt, or who had come from fear, have created more fear, and they want to go home. They've been listening to the dark side, and they are good at starting negative comments which none of that vast company seems to have any ability to diffuse, dissuade or prevent. They don't know God well.

Are they so damaged that they can't grasp the idea of a relationship with God? But then, their maturity level isn't very high, and negativity does come second nature to all of us. Discouragement is so easy to entertain, and quickly becomes a physical phenomenon perpetuated by hormones. It takes a choice to stop it. They obviously haven't practiced making choices. But they need to, and Adonai gives opportunities. Believing and obeying Him will grow them.

The majority of these people get a flunking grade in spiritual warfare. They don't seem to be able to trust at all—or even appreciate what they have.

196

And so, as often happens, spiritual ingratitude and unbelief give way to physical attack.

## The First Encounter with Physical War

Satan is counting on Israel's trust deficit, and sees an opening. "Look how these people talked to You and Moses, they have no right to protection," he says to Adonai. And what could Adonai say? It is part of Their Rules of Engagement. *If they are respectful and obedient you can't touch them.*[xxviii]

But clearly they had failed on both counts, and Satan stirs up the Amalekites. Yes, they are long lost relatives, Amalek was a son of Esau; but that doesn't matter when Satan inspires you to prove something. (This isn't their land, so they aren't protecting anything.) They are going to prove that Israel's God isn't real, or at least won't protect them. They mock the nations who are amazed with Israel's God, vowing to wipe Israel off the land.

So after the complaints, "We can't camp here! There is no water!" and Adonai provides once again, the first three-fourths are camping while the last fourth is still walking to the camp. The Amalekites attack the end of the company—the weak, the aged, the exhausted who can't go as fast.

Moses gets word and is furious! He rides out with his attendant, Joshua, and two other warriors and chases them off, yelling at them, "Come back tomorrow and fight like men!" and then they attend to the wounded.

Later he tells Joshua, "Choose the best warriors we have and tomorrow we will fight the Amalekites. I will stand on the top of the hill with the rod of God in my hand." The general in him takes over, counting on God to honor his prayers and come through for them. He wants both sides to know that the victory is Adonai's, but he doesn't expect they should do nothing.

So Joshua chooses men to fight and the next day Moses, Aaron, and Hur walk up the hill above the valley where the warriors are gathered for battle. (Hur in some traditional accounts in Miriam's husband—in others he's her son.)

The Amalekites come out to fight and as long as Moses is holding up his rod, Israeli warriors push them back. But his arms get tired. (That happens in less than an hour!) And when his arms go down the Amalekites chase them.

So Aaron and Hur come up with a plan. They seat Moses on a rock and Aaron and Hur stand on either side holding up Moses' hands with his rod until the sun goes down.

**Victory Comes with Blessing**

Joshua and his army overpower the Amalekites with their swords and God's blessing. Adonai wants to make it clear to Israel that even their best efforts require and depend on His blessings and intervention. They never have to worry as long as

He is helping them, and that comes for the asking. They can trust Him.

Adonai says to Moses, "Write this for a memorial in the book and read it later to Joshua to encourage him. I will utterly blot out the memory of the Amalekites from the earth." Evidently, Moses is keeping a journal (which later became the book of Numbers). And Joshua has already been picked as Moses' successor.

After that Moses built an altar and called the name of it Adonai-Nissi (the Lord is my banner) because without reason the Amalekites came against the banner of the Lord, therefore "He will have war with them their whole lives." This is not a judgment unless you think of judgement as discernment.

The Amalekites had made fun of the awe and fear that the other nations held for Israel's God, and planned to prove that it was all hype—just superstition. God saw this disrespect and defiance as irreversible. This was not a new thing for them. They have had plenty of time and opportunities to change. They had come from the same home generations back.

**"Write It Down"**

Adonai's direction to write brings up a very interesting point that first came up in the last episode. The Egyptians, by this date, had only progressed slightly past hieroglyphics as a way of

199

writing. However, it is known that hieroglyphics became a simple alphabet of 25 phonetic consonants, in the area around Sinai approximately 30 years before the Exodus. A group of Copper mining Canaanites who worked for Egypt are credited with making this language.[xxix] *Why would copper miners feel the need to create a language? I wondered. You don't need much for how much copper you sent where. Maybe to write letters?*

To me, it makes much more sense that Moses, wanting to write Job's story, and very well versed in the writing forms taught in Egypt, created a phonetic alphabet of consonants. He was much more likely to be motivated, and, no doubt, much more educated than Canaanite copper miners working for Egypt. And he was also used to keeping a journal of daily military campaigns as did his contemporary, Thutmose III, the one who succeeded Moses' Egyptian mother, Hatshepsut, as Pharaoh.

Add to that, our knowledge that Moses herded sheep on the Sinai Peninsula 40 years before the Exodus, and especially around Sinai, and it is much more likely that the copper miners were acquainted with Moses and learned the consonant alphabet from him who had already created it. Just my thoughts.

Chapter 18

# Reunited

## Exodus 18:1-19:16

*A glimpse of why Moses is called*
*"The meekest man who ever lived."*
*He was a model of teachability.*

"Master Moses!" calls a messenger, riding up, "Your family and Master Jethro are coming, and are a mile south on the road." Moses is excited and immediately turns over his work of settling disputes to Joshua, and runs out to meet them.

First he bows to this man who has become like a father to him, giving him customary respect. "God be with you. Are you all well?" he asks. And then after kissing and hugging all around, Jethro says,

"I've heard about all that God has done for you and your people, bringing them out of Egypt! So you were the deliverer all along!"

201

Moses smiles at him and looks down. By now he has learned a thing or two. "Adonai is their deliverer," he answers smiling at Jethro, "I'm just the guy He is using to keep them aware of that, to organize them, and to settle their disputes! And I would love to tell you all about what God has done for us! And how amazing He really is! Remember all those questions I used to ask you? I have seen a lot of answers!"

So they all go into Moses tent and he regales them with all the stories of what God did in Egypt with the plagues ending with the death of all the firstborn in Egypt, and how Pharaoh asked them to leave.

"That was an amazing night! In some ways, I was glad you weren't there," he says looking at Zipporah sitting next to him, and giving her shoulders a squeeze, "and in other ways I wish so much you all had been there!

"Did you see that pillar of cloud over Horeb as you came up? It covers Adonai. He has been with us since we left, and it was so great to see the people who had left home with their torches, put them out one by one, as they realized in awe that in His light they didn't need them. He has been so amazing! And crossing the Sea of Reeds was phenomenal! I wish you had seen that! Incredible! We walked on dry ground through walls of water, a huge one on the north, a smaller one on the south, with Him lighting the night and the water! Another time when the people started complaining, they saw Him in the desert, behind me, get so bright they couldn't look at Him! And that was in the daytime! It was just to show them He had heard them and that He isn't just a cloud but their God who cares and travels with them! He is so wonderful and good to them!"

And the others could see Moses glow as He spoke of Adonai.

"I wish I could have seen that!" said Jethro.

"Me too!" echoed Moses' sons.

"You will get to see His light at night while you are here." Moses smiled at them all, and went on to tell them how quail walked into the camp—enough for all of them to eat that night, and how the next morning there was manna—the bread of heaven.

"You will get to eat that while you are here. There will be enough for you too. It was crazy, when the men gathered it, some got more and some less, but when they measured it, it was exactly the amount needed for their families!

"And then just a few days ago they didn't want to camp here because there was no water! They were so angry with me I actually thought they would stone me, but Adonai had me strike a rock and He made water shoot out of it! A river came out of it! You will see that too! And then the Amalekites came!" And he tells them all about the attack and the battle Adonai helped them win.

"Oh man! Look what we missed!" shout his sons.

"You are here now! There will be plenty more to see, I am sure," laughs Moses.

"I am so happy for you and your experience with Adonai!" exclaims Jethro, laughing as well. "Praise to Adonai who has made good on all His words about you and delivered you from Egypt, and your people from their oppressors by your hand! Now I know for sure that Adonai is greater than all gods—especially since the Amalekites got what they deserved for their arrogance against Israel and our God!"

That evening Jethro presents a lamb to Moses that he brought for a thank offering for Adonai's goodness to them. And so they invite all the elders and Aaron to join them, in offering the lamb and eating together, in praise to Adonai.

**Jethro Gives Moses Advice**

The next day Jethro watches Moses sit and talk to the people who come and stand around Moses waiting to be heard, some of them waiting all day.

In the evening, the family is eating, and Jethro asks, "What is that you were doing for the people, with them standing around you all day?"

Moses explains, "The people come to me to inquire of God. When they have an issue or an argument, it comes to me and I judge between

204

them, so I am teaching them Adonai's laws—how He would look at their dispute."

"What you are doing is not good," observed his father-in-law. "You will surely wear yourself out, and exasperate the people who stand around waiting all day. The task is too heavy for one man; you can't do it by yourself.

"Listen, I will give you some advice, and may God be with you and help you hear me. Go ahead and teach the people about God—Their ways and Their laws; and show them how to walk with Them and follow Their ways. I'm sure after slavery they need the instruction.

"But find capable men from among your people— men who reverence God, men who love truth and hate bribery. Make them rulers over thousands, hundreds, fifties and tens. Then let them judge the people under them. The small things they can handle, the big ones they can take up to the next level and the major ones can be brought to you. But all the minor things they can decide. Make it easy on yourself, and let them help you bear the burden of all these people.

"If God agrees, and so commands you to do this, it will keep you from burning out, and all the people will quickly be able to go back to their places in peace."

Moses listened to Jethro and did everything he said. (No insecurity hinders his teachability

205

anymore!) He chose capable men and made them judges over a thousand, others heads over a hundred, and others over fifty and ten. They were available to hear the people at any time. The small cases they judged themselves, the bigger ones they took to a higher level, so that Moses only had to hear the hard cases.

With a sad but grateful heart, Moses let Jethro leave, and with tearful good-byes Jethro kissed his family and returned to his own home.

## God gets Israel Ready to Reunite with Him

The next day, Israel pulled up camp at Rephidim bedside Horeb and climbed the mountains leading up to Sinai. At times it seemed there was no way to go forward and then they would get closer and see the opening—a seemingly never-ending mass of humanity filing through narrow rocky passes. Moses had spent years here, bringing sheep up to this pasture when it dried up below in the summer. When they question, he smiles and assures them it will be worth it.

On the first day of June they walk through one such pass with rock walls towering on each side, when suddenly the narrow gorge opens into a wide-open, green meadow punctuated with thorn bushes, surrounded by mountain walls and the majesty of Sinai's face lit by the sun, rising from the green floor before them. The beauty takes their breath and they are happy to hear Moses direct them to start their usual camping formation at the spots their leaders indicate.

Family by family they pitch their tents, looking every now and again with awe at the huge rock walls surrounding their valley, their tents facing the massive peaks of Sinai.

The next morning, Adonai asks Moses to come up the mountain to speak with Him. So Moses goes. It seems like Moses hears God audibly—perhaps he always had since the burning bush—though it sounded like the people did also when His glory was shown to them in the Wilderness of Sin. Now it sounds different—God calls to him out of the mountain—like it is a bigger voice than usual—perhaps He wants him to see His majesty, and says,

"Tell the sons of Israel for Me, 'You have seen what I did to the Egyptians on your behalf, and how I carried you on eagles' wings and brought you to Myself.

"'Now then, if you listen closely to My voice and keep My covenant, then you will be My own special treasure from among all the people of the earth, for the whole earth is Mine. And you will be a kingdom of priests, distinctly raised up as My nation, to show the glory of My goodness.'

"These are the words which you shall speak to the children of Israel."

With very tender words God has Moses remind Israel's children of both the majesty of his protection at the Sea of Reeds, juxtaposing it with the carefulness of a mother eagle who dislodges her fledgling from the nest and then swoops underneath to catch him on her wings. He has shown himself mighty and loving in providing for their needs of deliverance, food, and water.

He presents like a parent, teaching, providing, yet almost more like a husband, as I am thinking about this covenant they will enter into. It's more like a wedding than an adoption or a business deal. And yet it is very majestic for a wedding! Maybe like marrying a king!

Moses comes down and calls for the elders of the people, and shares with them all the words Adonai has asked him to say to the people.

This is done in their smaller groups, so the people could talk about it and think about it, and they wouldn't be simply swayed by the masses. But the report that comes back from every elder is the same from each group. "Everything Adonai has said, we will do."

Moses is happy. He can't wait to see what Adonai's response will be. *It seems that finally these people are beginning to get it!* So he climbs back up the mountain and reports to Adonai what they said, and Adonai responds.

"I am going to come to you in a thick cloud so the people can hear Me when I speak, and believe that I talk with you forever. Tell the people to sanctify themselves by washing themselves and their clothes, and to be ready on the third day, and I will come down upon Mount Sinai in the sight of all the people.

"And you shall set boundaries around the bottom of the mountain and tell the people no one can go up into it or even touch the hills at the bottom of it. They must be careful not to touch it or they will die. And if any man or animal does touch it, no hand shall touch him or it, but he shall be stoned or shot through whether beast or man, so not to prolong death.

"When the trumpet sounds long, it will be safe to approach the mountain."

This is such an interesting directive. Obviously, if they touch the mountain, radiation or some energy we don't know about yet, will kill the person or animal, but not consume them. They will die, just not immediately, and God doesn't want anyone else contaminated. I've learned that the voltage upon entering, doesn't kill you, but when leaving your body it does. Since it can't be contained? Not enough receptors? So much we don't understand yet!

So Moses walks down and tells the people, "Be ready on the third day, wash your bodies and your

209

clothes, and do not have sex with your wives after that, as it will render you unclean."

He has the elders and leaders build a barrier around the bottom of the mountain. They didn't have caution tape, so I'm thinking they must have used all those thorn bushes that studded the valley. They would have cleared them to pitch their tents, and piled up thorn bushes would make an effective barrier.

Chapter 19

# The Awesome Covenant

## Exodus 19:16--Exodus 20:22

*"And he gave them His laws! Amazing!" –Moses*

On the morning of the third day the people awaken to thunder and lightning. There is no rain or wind, only excitement—this is no storm, this is God coming to meet with them and they have prepared to meet Him.

They quickly get ready and stand in front of their tents and watch as a dark cloud descends and covers the top of the mountain and then the whole 7,000 feet of Sinai—His granite podium.

There is a long blast of a trumpet that grows louder and louder and the people tremble as does the mountain. This is not their trumpet and they see no one blowing it.

211

Moses motions for the people to come and leads them to the bottom of the mountain. The top of Sinai is smoking because Adonai has descended upon it. All they see is fire. *The granite is on fire?* Moses thinks of the bush that was on fire but didn't burn. The smoke goes up like the smoke of a kiln. The mountain shakes greatly, as does the ground under their feet. The people tremble. And Moses says, "We are here, Lord. Even I am shaking."

Adonai answers him, saying, "Come up here, Moses," so Moses climbs up to the spot in the hills where he has talked with God before.

"Go down and warn the people to make sure they don't try to come up and see their God, and many of them die. Even the first born who have been set apart for Me must consecrate themselves, so they won't ignite."

Moses is perplexed, "But the people can't come up. You already warned us to put boundaries around the bottom so they can't, and we have done it." Moses thinks Adonai is repeating Himself unnecessarily. But God knows something Moses doesn't. Perhaps the first born or elders are thinking they have been set aside to God's service so they should be allowed to go up. And of course, they are curious. They would love to see God! And obviously have been considering it.

"Go down now. You and Aaron are to come back after I am finished speaking, but do not let the people come up or they will be killed by the energy."

So Moses climbs down; the people have had at least an hour break to stop shaking, the silence and stillness is filled with God's presence and feels full of meaning. They are more calm and able to listen.

Moses tells the elders and the people, "You must not think you need to climb the low hills to catch a glimpse of Adonai because His glory will kill you, even you first born unless you are first sanctified."

Can you even imagine what that was like! The majesty and grandeur! Seeing that granite mountain on fire, the trumpet bouncing off of rock walls, the ground shaking beneath your feet! (The ground moving makes incredible noise! We experienced it living fifteen miles from the epicenter of a 6.9 earthquake.)

If nothing impresses us as much as awe that must have been exactly God's plan. It isn't enough to know God's protection and provision, they need to know God's majesty—He is nothing like the multiplicity of gods in Egypt—their idols and animals which were credited with having power and doing things. This is the God who created these granite mountains with a word. Here is the perfect setting for Adonai to meet with them. He has provided an outdoor cathedral of stupendous dimensions and acoustics.

Moses takes his stand before the people, facing the mountain, his heart bursting to overflowing! *Now this is what You were talking about! Your promise has come true. How amazing Adonai would do this for them and for me! He wants them to know I know Him and speak for Him! This is their Deliverer, their Pursuer! This is our God!* Remember God had told him the sign of his calling was His presence and worshipping Him with all Israel on this mountain where He first spoke to him.

And then Adonai speaks out of the fire, his voice echoing off of the granite walls around the valley. And notice how He addresses them: "Thou" was used only to speak of God early in the English language—showing honor. Now He addresses them with such honor. Martin Buber has written a book titled *I and Thou* in which he speaks of this special relationship. One that is more than experiencing another as an object—it is a relationship encounter of delightful committed love (especially with God) free of angst because of God's covenant to love. (The next closest is marriage and children.) And so Adonai is setting them apart by having a relationship encounter with them—an experience of majesty and awe.

In graduate school I had a professor for a religion class who glowed peace. He reminded me of

214

Moses. When he talked about God, it was as if his face shown, literally. He read Hebrew fluently, and he told us that in the original language the Ten Commandments were positive. Their purpose being: *If you serve Me, you will be so secure, so content, so free in My love, you won't need to do any of the behaviors of the nations around you. You will be My Beloved, so satisfied.*

So imagine His huge majestic, musical voice speaking deliberately Their positive covenant, sounding something like:

**"I AM Adonai, your God, who brought you out of Egypt, out of bondage into the freedom of My love, and My Beloved will have no other gods but Me.**

**"You, My Beloved, will make no image of anything in the earth and call it god. You were made in *My* image. My Beloved won't bow down and worship anything but Me because that would degrade you. I am so anxious for you to be your true self that I won't share you with another god. All other "gods" take from you. But I even follow and oversee the children of those who don't want Me for four generations to see if I can find a way to reach them.**[xxx] **And I extend the blessings of those who love Me for thousands of generations.**

"You will not take on My Name or covenant with empty promises and pretend to belong to Me. I cannot protect you from the consequences of pretense.

"Remember the Sabbath day. It was a celebration in the Garden of Pleasure.[xxxi] Keep it as a special gift. You may pursue your interests on six days, but the seventh is the day of My rest. On that day you will not do your usual work, neither shall any person or animal in your household, because in six days I made your earth, and the seventh day all of us celebrated the end of creation together. God delighted in it, and set it apart for relationship. I come to be with you in a closer way on that day.

"Our covenant of honor extends to your father and mother so that I may keep you well and strong in the land I am giving you. They gave you life, and are due respect which is the basis of honor.

"You, My Beloved, won't need to kill for revenge or anger. Bring your anger or wounds of injustice to Me.

"You, My Beloved, won't need to use another man's wife for pleasure, I'll keep you satisfied with yours.

**"My Beloved won't need to steal; I will supply everything you need.**

**"My Beloved won't stoop to use falsehood against another. Lying makes you false.**

**"My Beloved won't even want your neighbors' wives, houses, servants, animals—nothing that belongs to him or her—because your God satisfies you. Come to Me and ask. I know you and your desires perfectly."**

And then God's voice stopped.

The people were awed, but they allowed it to make them afraid, especially when they realized how much they fought and created disputes with each other. *Can I be this? Can we do this?* They wondered. Self-realization hits hard in God's presence. But if you know Him, it's good pain. It feels like healing. Being in a love relationship makes doing right much easier.

I love this perspective of God's law which David, James, Paul, and others have called the perfect law of liberty. The Law of Love is the Law of Freedom! Everything in creation runs according to law, from the galaxies and planets in their orbits, to the gravity of this planet. If we are in harmony we aren't conscious of it, but if we defy it, either through intention or ignorance, it breaks us. Ignorance was their problem; Adonai helps by spelling out God's law succinctly. God is finished speaking, and the people back away.

Moses turns and sees them leaving. "Wait!" He calls loudly, his voice echoing too. "Why are you leaving?"

Shaken, the Israelites stop and tell their elders, "Tell Moses to speak to us instead of God and we will listen. But don't let God speak to us or we will die. He's too scary." How sad to miss more of His majesty!

The elders convey their message, and Moses speaks to the waiting people, "Don't be afraid, God has come Himself to speak His covenant so that His awe may produce reverence in you and keep you from doubting or disbelieving Him."

After Moses spoke to them, the people went back and stood at their tents, while Moses climbed up into the low mounds right where the darkness began.

How was this different from Adonai's presence in the cloud? He was in the cloud as Michael the archangel because sometimes Moses calls Him the angel of the Lord, referring to the cloud (14:19). But this is God coming to earth without disguise—without becoming human or angelic first!

What care He has to take not to destroy us! Moses and the author of Hebrews both call God a consuming fire. [xxxii] Here we are seeing exactly what they were referring to. This is the only time

God comes to earth without disguise. The majesty and awe of God are life-changing and important to understand and experience—even the little bit we can. Don't back away from it!

Adonai speaks with Moses for over an hour and gives him all the rules that simplify the covenant into behavior for all their situations. How kind of him to meet them where they are! They are like children acting on impulse and he shows them a better way.

Moses comes down and calls them all together and reads all of God's instructions to the people. Rules regarding servants, quarrels that result in injury, the penalty for human trafficking, responsibility and restitution for loss or injury, how to handle theft, and when to use a death penalty. Adonai also warns them not to mistreat widows and orphans, and gives them rules for lending and taking pledges. And then He outlines what it means to live as His special people in everything from eating to planting to treating outsiders to taking bribes.

Moses also reads Adonai's directions for celebrating three festivals a year, ending with, "I will send My Angel before you to protect and guard you on the way to the place I have prepared. Pay attention to Him and listen and obey. Do not rebel or provoke him for He will not excuse transgression, for My Name is in Him (Michael means "like God").[xxxiii]

"But if you listen and obey, I will be an enemy to your enemies, and when I bring you into your land I will drive them out. But you must not bow to any of their gods or do their works, but break down the pillars and images to their gods.

"You serve Me, and I will bless your food and water and take sickness away from you. No woman shall miscarry or be barren. (Here is a reason to believe that disease comes from diet!)

"I will send My terror before you and throw your adversaries into confusion and make them run from you. I will send hornets before you to drive out the people from your promised land. I will not drive them out in one year or the wild animals will multiply against you. [xxxiv] Little by little I will eliminate them until you are numerous enough to take possession of the land.

"I will set your borders from the Red Sea to the Sea of the Philistines and from the wilderness to the River Euphrates, for I will deliver the inhabitants into your hand. You shall make no covenant with them or their gods. You shall not live with them in your land, or intermarry, for if you serve their gods it will be a trap to you, and break our covenant."

After Moses finishes reciting to the people (Ruach helping him remember, I'm sure), all the people say with one voice, "All the words which Adonai has spoken we will do."

That evening Moses writes all the rules he had spoken to the people and afterwards Adonai speaks and says,

"Tomorrow morning you are to gather the people and confirm the covenant with them just as we talked about. Then come up to Me in the mount, you, Aaron, his sons Nadab and Abihu, and seventy of the elders of Israel, and worship from afar. You alone are to approach Me, but the others may not draw near, nor any of the people."

God is so inclusive that this was simply a protective measure. Remember They even allowed anyone who wanted to leave Egypt to come with them ("the mixed multitude). Even though They knew Satan would use those people to try and corrupt Theirs.

God's plan reaches out to anyone who is interested, anyone who responds to Their hearts of goodness and kindness. They especially wanted to show Their character of love and kindness to the watching world. That was the reason for a chosen people—having a nation that Adonai could lead and though whom He could show His goodness to the world. He would be their King and later their ransoming Messiah.

The whole idea was to have a people whom He could bless beyond belief, so that other nations or individuals would want to know and serve their benevolent, wise God. To show how superior was their God to idols, Adonai would make them the head of all nations—a great power for good and blessing in the world. And His light would reach everyone in the world through Israel. They only had to agree to be His covenant people.

Chapter 20

# Blessed Beyond Belief

## Exodus 20:22-24:18

*In confirming their covenant the people said, "All the words of Adonai we will do." They should have said, "How can we do that?"*

The next morning Moses wakes up before sun rise. *This is the day we confirm the covenant and then I get to take Aaron and the elders up the mountain to worship!* He feels excitement and expectancy as he thinks *then Adonai said I get to meet with Him alone!* He remembers the grandeur of yesterday and shivers.

*I can hardly wait! I wonder what being alone with Him will be like? What will we do? Will the people be ok down here? God has told me I will be gone for some time. Miriam and the women with her are going to lead them in worship while the large group is gone; and then Aaron and Hur will be in*

223

*charge.* He sees Zipporah sleeping beside him. It has been wonderful having her again, and he feels very protective of her. He has told her he gets to spend some time alone with God. *But what about my family? They don't know many people but Aaron's family. I can't worry about them. That's Ruach's job. Take care of them, please.*

He's dresses and slips out and builds an altar out of stones which he finds at the bottom of the mountain, just outside the barrier. Then he finds larger stones—12 of them—and sets them up as pillars. The people have been told to meet with him right after breakfast. It's the day after Sabbath but Adonai had said their Manna would last. There will be no manna gathering this morning. This is a high day!

Twelve young men, worthy first-borns selected by their tribes yesterday, who are spiritually minded and able to handle the animals being sacrificed, present themselves to Moses just as he is finishing. They each bring a lamb and an ox to offer as instructed.

"Are you ready?" Moses smiles at them. *Fine young men,* he thinks, telling each where he should go and then all of them the procedure to follow. He blows the ram's horn. The leaders and people are assembling behind them.

After the young men are each beside his altar, he lays his lamb for the whole congregation on the

224

main altar and they do the same on their pillar. He takes half of the blood and pours it in a basin and the other half he pours out on the altar, signifying God's acceptance of them.

Then he reads all the words of the covenant again. I will skip the Ten because they are in the last chapter, (but you may notice, the first three are repeated as one before the rules are read). And since the civil laws were written in ancient Hebrew, I will simplify them and what I don't understand, even after researching them, I will give the consensus.

It is noteworthy that they are more equitable and gentle than the contemporary Hammurabi code,[xxxv] which is acclaimed for its ancient wisdom.

But observe, all through, they are completely based on respect. God did not allow disrespect anywhere. Remember that the Lawgiver, later as Jesus, simplified them into two laws: love for God and love for man.[xxxvi]

So Moses reads the Ten Commandments and the civil laws for the second time beginning with a prelude combining the first three as follows:

"Adonai says, 'You have seen and heard Me speak to you from heaven, so do not make gods of gold and silver to worship alongside Me. You can make an altar of earth or rough stones for your offerings, but do not chisel or engrave them or make a huge

225

altar with steps going up to it so that it becomes your shrine and your shame.[xxxvii]

'Everywhere I ask you to erect an altar, do it simply without using tools on it, as your embellishment profanes it; and I will come and bless you just as I always have.'

In other words for us, 'Come to me as you are, without trying to make yourself better. Your works profane the gift of yourself.'

If you want the full effect jump back and read the Ten Commandments again in the last chapter. Then Moses read the rules that came from the Ten.

'These are the judgments the elders will use for discernment. Teach them to the people.

'If a Hebrew sells himself as a slave he shall go free after six years of service without paying for his freedom. If he desires to stay because his wife and children are your servants, then put a ring in his ear in your doorway to show he has chosen to serve you for life.

'If a man sells his daughter, she is to be bought as a wife. If her husband decides she doesn't please him or takes another wife, he must give her a wife's rights; if not, she goes free. He may not sell her to a foreign person or nation, but may allow her to be redeemed by her nearest relative. If he gives her to his son, he must give her the rights of a daughter.

'If a man kills another, he must forfeit his own life. If it was an accident then I will appoint a place for him to run to safety. Also, anyone who repeatedly curses or strikes his father or mother incurs the death penalty.

'If a man hits another in a quarrel, and the man gets better, the perpetrator must pay for his time off and make sure of his recovery.

'Responsibility is required for every loss or injury whether to a slave (he goes free) or a miscarriage (whatever the father demands). But to an equal you will pay just compensation (eye for eye, tooth for tooth). For an animal, sometimes you will replace it, sometimes pay, as the judge discerns. If an animal is destructive more than once, the owner must pay for it. If he gores someone more than once, the ox is killed and the owner forfeits his life if the person dies. If someone digs a well or a pit and leaves it open, and another animal falls in, he must replace it.

'Responsibility for theft is required at 4 to one for sheep, and 5 oxen for one ox as this was clearly planned. If a thief breaks in before light and is killed there is no guilt—his intent is considered murder. If it is light there is bloodguilt on the owner/killer. The thief who is unable to restore double, must be sold to pay back his theft.

'Responsibility for livestock on another man's land, or someone setting a fire, must be monetary pay back or in goods. In cases of stolen goods, both parties must come before the judge, and the guilty one pay back double. In claims of safe-keeping for another or loans made that went bad, the judge will decide.

'If a man seduces a virgin and has sex with her he must pay her bride price and marry her. If her father refuses to give her to him, he must still pay the bride price.

'The death penalty applies to sorcerers, sex with an animal, and anyone sacrificing to another god (which is treason).

'You must not mistreat or exploit outsiders, for you were outsiders in Egypt, and know what that is like. You must not mistreat widows and orphans. If you do, and they cry to Me, your wives will become widows and your children orphans.

'If you lend money to your people, you are not to charge interest. If you take a cloak from a poor man as a pledge, you shall return it at sunset so he has a blanket. If he cries to Me about you, I will hear him for I am gracious.

'Don't curse God or your leaders. Don't be stingy with your water or your wine, and don't eat animals that have been killed or torn by another animal in the field. You may feed it to your dogs.

'Dedicate your firstborn sons and sheep and cattle to Me. Be different from the nations around you for My sake.

'Don't pass on gossip. Don't follow the crowd or link up with an evil person or give a false testimony and pervert justice, even for the poor. Don't accept bribes, or sway a verdict to slay an innocent man.

'Do not plant your fields on the seventh year, but let the land rest. And let the poor and the animals eat what grows. And the same for your vineyards and orchards.

'Just as you work six days and rest the seventh day so your servants and animals may be refreshed as well as the traveler with you. Pay attention to My words, and make no mention of other gods, even their names.'"

And then he repeated the observances of the feasts and the blessings of being Adonai's people as written in the last chapter.

After Moses finishes reading the civil laws, all the people answer as one voice and say, "All that Adonai has spoken, we will do and obey."

This is the second time they have heard it in two days—likely none of them can read, although Moses is probably teaching the leaders. Time has been given in between the first and second reading so the people can consider His laws and decide if they want to be God's people, make Him their king, and make a covenant with Him. They are free to leave, and they aren't far from Midian or so far from Egypt that they couldn't return.

No doubt, there are a few in "the mixed multitude" that God would have leave—a few interspersed by Satan to bring down the rest. (Or why would they need a law against sorcerers?) But God is inclusive, and will not exclude any who choose to be there.

Then Moses put his fingers in the other half of the blood in the basin and sprinkled it on the elders and the young men and the leaders of the tribes standing in the front. This signified all the people's acceptance.

"This is the blood of the covenant which Adonai has cut with you, for agreeing to all His words."

Then Moses says, "Aaron and Aaron's sons and the original elders have been called up to the mountain to worship God while you worship in the valley. Miriam and the women will lead the congregation in singing."

So Moses, Aaron, his sons, and seventy elders walk up to the spot on the mounds where Moses talked with God. They arrive and see the shape of a man in light brighter than the sun and his feet standing on pavement that looked like translucent sapphire—clear as air. He did not approach them or touch them, but they sat down and ate and drank in His presence.

Can you imagine how that felt! Being in the very Presence! Even if all you see is light—like a dream of heaven I had a year ago—everything was bright light, and a wonderful feeling of no condemnation—pure freedom and a feel good I never wanted to leave.

Then they hear God's soft musical voice, "Moses, come up to me on the mountain and stay there until I call you to give you two stone tablets on which I have written My Law so you can teach the people."

Moses and Joshua stand up, "Wait here until we turn back and wave. Then go on down to the people, and don't come looking for us; we will come back. Aaron and Hur are in charge; if you have any problems go to them."

Joshua and Moses climb up farther and turn around and wave, and then step into the dark cloud of Presence. There they waited for six days in prayer and meditation. Did Moses know he was preparing to withstand the glory? Probably, but he had no idea how long it would take. On the seventh day (Sabbath) Adonai called to Moses; and Moses went into the glory—the presence of God. It looked to Israel like the mountain was on fire again.

Even God's friend, Moses, had to wait in God's presence for six days to be able to move in closer and speak with God and not be destroyed by what looked like consuming fire from the bottom. But isn't it amazing that a broken human could be in

231

that unveiled fire of glory and live! This was the special something Abba wanted for him.

Moses stayed there for 40 days and 40 nights with Adonai. During that time Joshua stayed at the edge of the cloud fed by manna and drinking from a mountain stream. He and Moses had done that for the six days they waited on God, but when Moses was in the mountain with Adonai, there was no need for food or water. (He didn't even think about it.) God's glory is that powerful.

(It also makes me think of the 40 days Jesus spent in the wilderness. Was he caught up in the glory of God, reviewing his mission until the end of the time, like Moses was?)

God had set them up to be the premier nation: blessed beyond belief over every people in the whole world if they would trust Adonai. It was their habit to look at their circumstances in fear, or look at their ability in despair. **God told them repeatedly, He would always do and be what they needed—all He needed was their trust and request for help.** There is no shame in admitting weakness. In fact, it is a great advantage to know and admit your weakness: it usually disarms others and makes you strong. Admitting weakness and asking for help allows Ruach, Adonai and Abba to work. And They are stronger than anyone or anything!

This is the 5<sup>th</sup> book in the *Love's Playbook* series which takes you through the Bible looking for the description of God given in 1John 1:5..."in Him there is no darkness at all." If we look at all the bits and pieces, especially the cosmic ones, we see a picture of God that is always, and in all ways, good.

*Love's Playbook 6 will* cover Exodus 25-40 and Leviticus, Numbers and Deuteronomy.

Other books by this author:

The Worst Evil—Losing Yourself

Love's Playbook:
1 The Real Story of Cosmic
   Love &War
2 The Romance Begins
3 The Perception of Failure
4 Beyond Suffering

# About the Author

"If there is a loving God, why did all those horrible things happen to me as a child?" was the most frequent question Arla Caraboolad was asked in her first teaching position. She was 22. The setting was the California prison for women.

The question began a search for answers.

How much was God involved in life on earth? Was He responsible for the bad that happened to us as well as the good?

Whatever was "evil" anyway? How much of it came from us, and how much of it came from some other place? And

was God really responsible?

Many years as a parent and step-parent and twenty-five years as a Family-Systems Therapist have aided that exploration. Because God was real to her, and important, and because questions about life and self are usually all tangled up with questions about God, her need-to-know grew.

Forty-five years later this search and research have formed a background for writing this series, and especially this book on finding strength in weakness. But fifty years as a Bible student, seventeen of them formal studies, constructed the platform.

Website: http://Godhelps.net

# Notes

[i] Josephus. <u>Antiquities ii, 9. 6</u>

[ii] Keil and Delitzsch. <u>Commentary on the Old Testament, Vol 1</u>. Grand Rapids: Eerdmans Publishing Co., 1978, p 428.

[iii] Francis Nichol ed. et al. <u>SDA Bible Commentary</u>, Vol 1. Washington DC: Review and Herald Publishing Asso., 1953, p 499-500, 503.

[iv] Ibid, p. 525.

[v] Ibid, p. 497-8.

[vi] Ibid, p 502.

[vii] Ibid, p.502.

[viii] Ibid, p 504.

[ix] Caraboolad. <u>Love's Playbook</u> vol.4. Beyond Suffering. The story of Job is told in detail in episode 4, so here it is just referred to for the effect it had on Moses, its author.

[x] Keil and Delitzsch. Ibid. p 437.

[xi] Ibid, p 438-9.

[xii] Adonai is the Hebrew name typically translated Jehovah and sometimes Yahweh. I prefer Adonai, as does the Tree of Life Version (TLV) translated by the Messianic Jewish Family Bible Society--the version most used throughout this series.

[xiii] Exodus 12:23 makes it clear that God allowed Satan (the Destroyer according to Hebrews 2:14) to destroy the firstborn.

[xiv] See note #9.

[xv] Nichol. Ibid, p 530.

[xvi] Ibid, p 532

[xvii] In addition to Exodus 12:23 and Hebrews 2:14, Satan is called the destroyer in Isaiah 10:20 and 33:1.

[xviii] Entropy comes from evil and is the law that rules on earth: the Law of Sin and Death known here as entropy—the tendency of everything toward chaos and decay.

[xix] Romans 1 says three times that God's wrath is giving us up to our own way. Isaiah and Jeremiah alone have over 30 references to God's wrath being giving people and nations over to the enemy.

[xx] Nichol. Ibid, p 542.

[xxi] See endnote xi on Exodus 12:23

[xxii] Mahoney, Timothy. Patterns of Evidence Exodus. Film, 2016.

[xxiii] Josephus. Ibid, 16.6.

[xxiv] Revelation 15:3

[xxv] Nichol. Ibid, p 554.

[xxvi] Mazar, Benjamin, chairman. <u>Views of the Biblical World,</u> Vol 1. Arco Publishing Co: New York , NY. p 145.

[xxvii] White, E. The Story of Patriarchs and Prophets. Mountain View, CA: Pacific Press Publishing Asso. 1913, p 294.

[xxviii] See Job 1-2. Or read episode 4 in this series.

[xxix] Nichol. Ibid, p 586.

[xxx] This is in agreement with what God said to Abraham in Gen. 15:16 about the Amorites not being ready for handing over to the enemy for 400 years. Also the Hebrew rendering of "visiting" could be "overseeing".

[xxxi] The original meaning of Eden is pleasure—see Strong's Concordance.

[xxxii] Deuteronomy 4:24, and Hebrews 12:29

[xxxiii] Exodus 32:34; 33:14; Isaiah 63:9…See episode 1.

[xxxiv] Nichol. Ibid, p 629, When the Northern ten tribes were dispossessed the lions increased and preyed upon the remnant.

[xxxv] Nichol. Ibid, pp 617-619.

[xxxvi] The Lawgiver being Adonai who offered himself as God's remedy and 1500 years later became Jesus, Matthew 22:36-40.

[xxxvii] Keil and Delitzsch. Ibid, p 128.

Made in the USA
San Bernardino, CA
03 October 2018